Faithful UNTIL Death

THE STORY OF
Necati Aydin,
A TURKISH
MARTYR
FOR CHRIST

Wolfgang Haede

Living Sacrifice Book Company
Bartlesville, OK 74005

Faithful Until Death: The Story of Necati Aydin, A Turkish Martyr for Christ

Living Sacrifice Book Company
P.O. Box 2273
Bartlesville, OK 74005-2273

The original German edition was published as *Mein Schwager – ein Märtyrer. Die Geschichte des türkischen Christen Necati Aydin*. Copyright © 2009 Neufeld Verlag Schwarzenfeld, www.neufeld-verlag.com.

ISBN 978-0-88264-055-6

Translated into English by Neal Newman

Edited by Lynn Copeland

Cover, page design, and production by Genesis Group

Printed in the United States of America

Unless otherwise indicated, Scripture references are from the *New King James* version, © 1979, 1980, 1982 by Thomas Nelson Inc., Publishers, Nashville, Tennessee.

Scripture quotations designated NASB are from the *New American Standard Bible*, © 1960, 1962, 1963, 1968, 1971, 1972, 1973, 1975, 1977 by the Lockman Foundation, La Habra, California.

To Necati,
who is among the host of the martyrs
who "did not love their lives to the death,"
and who stand before the throne
of God Almighty

Notes on Turkish Spelling & Pronunciation

Names: The names of some individuals have been changed for their protection. The Turkish names of people and places have not been transliterated but have been given in their original forms, with the exception of Turkish letters which do not exist in English.

Pronunciation: The name Necati Aydin is pronounced "Ne-jah'-tee Eye-dunn," and the name Semse is pronounced "Shem'-se." In the name Ugur the "g" is not spoken, so the name is pronounced approximately "Ew-oar." The name of Necati and Semse's son, Elisa Günes, is pronounced "E-leesh'-a Goon-esh'."

Contents

Introduction

MOST CHRISTIANS in the West today are probably above suspicion when it comes to having an inordinate longing for suffering. Tangible success and effortless achievement seem to be the norms even for spiritual life. At the same time, however, I notice a sort of longing for martyrs. People like Dietrich Bonhoeffer and Martin Luther King are highly respected.

I am convinced that many people in Western countries also want to have visions and goals that are worth living and dying for—and mentors who do not just philosophize about things but practice them. We need martyrs!

In 2007 three men devoted their lives—very clearly as Christians. They were faithful to the very last breath. Their deaths were a continuation of their lives, and even in their type of death they resembled "sacrificial lambs." They were genuine followers of their Lord Jesus Christ.

I was also in this event; the murderers wanted to kill me also, and one of those killed was my relative, the Pastor Necati Aydin—my brother-in-law, a martyr.

April 18, 2007

FOR AS LONG as I live, I will probably never forget this day. A meeting with other pastors had just ended in Kadiköy, the ancient Chalcedon which is now part of Istanbul—Turkey's largest city with a population of about 13 million. I bought a bus ticket for the 75-minute trip to Izmit, where my wife, Janet, and I, with our nine-year-old daughter, had been working for just over five years to plant a Turkish Protestant church.

I called Janet to tell her when I would be home, and she said, "Wolfgang, I have just spoken to Semse. There has been an attack on Necati's office at Zirve Publishing in Malatya. She doesn't know exactly what has happened."

Immediately I tried to reach Necati by phone. He was married to my wife's younger sister, Semse, and at age thirty-five was pastor of a small Evangelical church in Malatya, in eastern Turkey. He didn't answer his cell phone, but I had two additional phone numbers for him, and when I called them they also rang unanswered.

I began to have an ominous fear when there was no answer.

I called Semse and she sounded amazingly calm. "I have been informed by others that the office of Zirve Publishing has been shot at," she said. "I have the TV on now. We simply need to pray."

I had to board my bus. As the reports started pouring in, Christians in Istanbul called me. I heard from David, an American missionary, then Sara, the wife of a pastor in Istanbul, then Caner, a Turkish brother. Each of them gave me the information that one of the many TV stations had printed on the screen: "Four Christians have been murdered."

"Necati is probably among them."

"Good news: one TV station has just given the names of four others."

"One of the murderers is dead."

"I'm sorry, it has just been confirmed that Necati was among them."

Speaking on the phone is actually forbidden on the bus, but the bus attendant seemed to notice that something unusual had occurred, so he allowed me to.

I felt as if I had been transported into a different world. My first reaction to such terrible news was: "*Isa'nin adi yüceltilsin!*—May the name of Jesus be exalted!"

When I arrived home, brothers and sisters from our small church were already gathered in our living room. When someone passes away, Turks immediately hurry to the home of the relatives or close acquaintances to comfort them, to not leave them alone, to help with practical chores, to simply be there. In that moment, I was thankful for this aspect of Middle Eastern culture.

The rough facts of the terrible incident had become known. We would receive more details in the hours and days to come.

On the morning of April 18, two Turkish men, Emre Günaydin and Abuzer Yildirim, came into the office of Zirve Publishing. Supposedly the men wanted to learn more about the Christian faith, as they had a few times in the weeks before.

Necati wanted to use this opportunity to tell them about Jesus, even though he had previously told his wife that he did not think the men's interest was very genuine. Necati did not know that they had brought two knives and a blank pistol with them this time.

Besides Necati, Tilmann Geske was also in the office. He was a forty-six-year-old German Christian who had been living in Turkey for years, and aside from his job as an English teacher, he had been assisting in the Protestant church in Malatya, which Necati led. In addition, Ugur Yüksel, age thirty-two, came to the office. He was from the nearby city of Elazig. He had been working at Zirve Publishing for about a year.

According to Turkish hospitality, tea was served. After a short conversation the doorbell rang. Emre explained that he wanted to have three additional friends there for the discussion. Then Hamit Ceker, Cuma Özdemir, and Salih Gürler came in and joined the three Christians. They had also brought three more large knives, adequate clothesline, and plastic gloves—all of which they had hidden in plastic bags. Besides this they had two blank pistols, which at first glance are difficult to distinguish from real weapons even by experts.

Even today the exact sequence of events for the massacre that followed has not been sufficiently reconstructed. Later in court the murderers tried to accuse each other and gave contradictory testimony. A rough outline of the crime seems to be:

The young men threatened Necati, Ugur, and Tilmann with the pistols and knives. Then all three Christians had their arms and legs bound and were thrown face down to the floor. The three Christians were verbally abused, "interrogated," and most likely commanded to reject their beliefs.

When the judge asked the murderers if the victims had made no replies, the record of their testimony shows how peaceful the three must have been even in the face of death. The record also shows that Ugur called out to Christ as his brothers were murdered.

The record of their testimony shows how peaceful the three must have been even in the face of death.

One of the murderers tried to strangle Necati with clothesline. When Semse heard about this later, she was appalled, because one of Necati's greatest fears during his life was that of being in close quarters and being unable to breathe.

All three were then tortured; they were stabbed and kicked all over their bodies. Later the official autopsy report would show strangulation marks and six stab or cut wounds for Necati, sixteen stab or cut wounds for Tilmann, and fourteen for Ugur.

The murderers finished their cruelty by kneeling on the backs of their victims, cutting their carotid arteries, and then letting them bleed to death.

Gökhan, a Turkish apprentice in the Malatya church, and his wife, Özge, arrived at the door of the publishing house just before 1:00 p.m. After Gökhan realized that the office door was locked and that the key was still in the lock on the other side, he tried to reach his brethren in the faith on his cell phone. Necati and Tilmann could no longer answer; they were already dead.

The murderers forced Ugur to speak into the phone: "We're at the Golden Apricot Hotel for a meeting. You can meet us there." Ten days earlier they had celebrated Easter in a room they had rented at the hotel, but what could they have been doing there at that time? Ugur's voice sounded unusual and pained; Gokhan called the police.

As the police were nearing the crime scene, Ugur's throat was cut. Despite the transfusion of 50 units of blood, he died as a result of his wounds at 6:30 p.m.

In trying to run away from the police, the main suspect, Emre Günaydin, fell from the fourth-story balcony. He was the fourth of those who had been reported to have died. He was only critically injured, however, and weeks would pass before he could be questioned. The other four murderers were arrested at the scene of the crime.

The police carried the black-shrouded bodies of Necati and Tilmann out of the building. The picture of Ugur, who was bleeding to death yet still raised his hand to show his worst wounds, was broadcast throughout the world.

The motive of the murderers is clear: they viewed missions as a danger for their religion and their country and they wanted to hinder it. If they had not been caught in the act, they later testified, they would have traveled to Izmit in western Turkey. There they wanted to get Pastor Wolfgang, the brother-in-law of Necati Aydin, out of the way, and thereby "break two legs of missions." I am Pastor Wolfgang.

> *There they wanted to get Pastor Wolfgang out of the way, and thereby "break two legs of missions." I am Pastor Wolfgang.*

The next day we flew to Malatya in eastern Turkey. A trip by bus would have taken about fourteen hours. Christians from various areas of Turkey had already gathered in the apartment of my sister-in-law Semse, in support of the widows and the small Christian church there. In addition to these, television and newspaper reporters came in from time to time. The murders in Malatya had become a media spectacle.

The days preceding Necati's burial on April 21 were full of moving and harrowing impressions. Tilmann was to be buried on Friday in Malatya as his family wished. But it proved to be very difficult to find workers to dig the grave. Burying a Christian on Friday, the Islamic day of worship, did not seem to be fitting for them. In the end, Christians who had come from other cities to mourn with the widows began to dig a grave in the hard ground of the Christian graveyard.

Necati's funeral

Necati's oldest brother came in from Izmir. However, instead of just expressing his condolences, he demanded, in the name of his whole family, that the corpse of his brother be buried according to Islamic rite. Semse, of course, rejected this demand.

In the end Necati's casket, which was brought to Izmir, was too large to be pushed through the security scanner at the airport. But the officials were very abrupt and did not want to take any shortcuts with respect to the security procedures. A Christian who was a witness to this remarked bitterly, "They are not only afraid of the living, they are even afraid of the dead."

For me April 18 and the following days were very peculiar. I was hurt bitterly by the departure of my dear brother-in-law, but at the same time I felt especially near to heaven. In those days it was as if time had stopped and that a small glimpse of another world had been permitted, the world of God in which different standards and values are valid. Three lives had been brutally extinguished in their primes—but from God's perspective they were not extinguished, but rather raised up into glory. They seemed to have been slaughtered senselessly—but similar to the way the blood of Jesus brought salvation to the world, the blood of these men would become, as the church father Tertullian put it, the "seed of the Church" in Turkey.

The murderers appeared to have succeeded in destroying the great potential of a future effective ministry for Jesus, which Necati possessed both as a leader and as one of the few committed Christians in Turkey. However, "a grain of wheat [that] falls into the ground and dies" (John 12:24) would bring more spiritual fruit than would have been possible in even thirty or forty more years of evangelistic and pastoral ministry.

Typically Turkish?

WHEN MY WIFE and I first met Necati in the summer of 1996, we did not have the faintest inkling that the slight young man before us would become the first martyr of the Turkish church since the establishment of the Turkish Republic.

My sister-in-law, Semse, was getting ready to become engaged to Necati. We had come from Germany to Izmir, the ancient Smyrna, in western Turkey for our summer vacation. Semse had already told us about Necati, but now we were to meet him personally at a picnic.

Necati was twenty-four then, but he seemed younger. We realized how nervous he was about being "inspected" by us. Our first impression was that he was a very polite young Turk, who received us respectfully as being the "elders in the family." However, he tended to be shy, a little "super intellectual," and not sure of himself. His vocabulary was riddled with old Arabic words that I could not understand. The use of such terms indicated that he

Necati and Semse

came from a strict Islamic background and also that he consciously identified with it. Modern, more Western-oriented Turks tend to avoid the old religious language.

I cannot remember the details about our conversation at the picnic—but rather that my wife and I were not very sure about the relationship between Necati and Semse. Necati was four years younger than Semse, he had come to accept Jesus through her witness, and we could not tell how grounded he was in the faith. Especially in Turkish culture, should not the man be the strongest and the leader? Had he clearly left his old beliefs and really found in Jesus the foothold for his life? Only then would he and his future family be able to survive the special challenges that Christians in Turkey must face.

After our summer vacation Janet and Semse had long telephone conversations. Janet generally warned her younger sister to be careful in the relationship.

Later we learned more about Necati. Many aspects of his life were typical of life in Turkey today. For decades Turkey has undergone sudden and major changes, part of which is the migration of the population within the country and into foreign countries. Necati's family had also been affected by this.

His father, Enver Aydin, was a low-level government worker. He brought two daughters from his deceased wife into the marriage with Necati's mother, Bahar. Three sons and two daughters later, Necati was the last to be born in 1972.

The Aydin family lived in Hinis, located in the eastern Turkish province of Erzurum. The father's roots are further to the northeast. He is Circassian; his forefathers came from the multi-ethnic Caucasus.

The Ottoman Empire, out of which modern-day Turkey was formed, consisted of numerous ethnic groups, whose traces one can still find among many who describe themselves as Turks.

In 1975 the father, who was then much older than sixty and in retirement, decided to move to western Turkey with his wife and children. Many from eastern Turkey hoped to find a better future for their children in the major cities of western Turkey. After a brief stay in Eskisehir, the family finally settled in Menemen in the province of Izmir in the Aegean region. Necati would spend his childhood there.

As the youngest in the family, Necati was cared for in a special way by his mother, and he liked sitting on her lap. Necati's character, however, seems to have been nearer his father's. He described him as a very meek person,

Necati as young man, as a child, and in school uniform

whom he never heard curse—something that is unusual for Turkish men.

The living standards in which young Necati grew up were average for Turks at that time. The father bought a small house from his savings, which protected his family from the oppressive rental costs experienced by other families. The family at large was not extremely poor, but they always just scraped by, and each member had to contribute what he could for his expenses.

So as a child Necati earned money as a shoe shiner and by doing other simple tasks. In his youth he worked in construction with his older brothers during the summer months. Although he was small and thin, he lugged the heavy bucket of plaster from the mixer to the fourth or fifth story of the building. Sometimes he also worked with a finish carpenter and had to carry wooden doors weighing not much less than he did. The hard work he did as a child could have caused the back problems that afflicted him in later life.

During that time in his life Necati learned to be an industrious and hard worker in order to support others. Even after he began his career as a bookkeeper, he still contributed to the support of the family and enjoyed buying presents for his nephews and nieces.

As is the case for many in Turkey, the family is also the anchor of Necati's life. In the family, by which the extended family is generally meant, one could find recognition and security, but was also expected to display unconditional loyalty to them. One's earnings were always brought to the family, and important decisions, such as those regarding one's career or marriage, were not made without the approval of the family head.

Necati never thought of breaking out of this system. He greatly respected not only his parents, but also his older siblings—and this is generally valued highly in the culture. Necati took this respect more seriously than most. Semse said later that he would always express deference to his next oldest brother, who was but one year older.

Only one who understands Necati's background can begin to imagine what it later meant for him to be alienated and rejected because of his faith in Jesus. At the same time, as far as I am concerned, he was an exemplary representative of the positive traits of a genuine Turk. That is the tragic irony of the life story of my brother-in-law.

Because of his conversion from Islam to Christianity, Necati was branded as a traitor of his Turkish ethnicity by his own family and many of his countrymen. Yes, Necati's life was changed by Christ, but he retained the good aspects of the Turkish lifestyle and his great love for Turkey. He even refined these features of Turkish culture under the influence of the gospel. Because of this he was a real representative to me of the special gifts that God has given the Turkish people.

Necati's respect for those older than him was something I could experience personally. I was a few years older than Necati, and since I was also his brother-in-law, I took on the position of an older brother, or *abi* (ah-bee), for him. He always called me not just by my name but "Wolfgang *Abi*," that is, big brother Wolfgang. He listened attentively when I spoke and he greatly respected my opinion. Even later, as Necati's ministry grew and he "surpassed" me in his position in God's Kingdom, he never put aside his respect for me.

Not to harm another by disrespect or by direct verbal attack is something that is highly valued by Turks, because a person's honor and reputation are very important. Necati was a master at politely packaging even warranted criticism. I am sure that he not only clearly presented the good news of Jesus Christ in his many evangelistic discussions, but that he also never mocked or disrespected the faith of those he spoke with (that is, Islam).

As a Christian, Necati did not live in financial abundance. As a representative of "good Turkish characteristics," however, he was especially generous. I remember well the "fights" we had over who would pay the bill when our families would go out to eat together. In Turkish culture this struggle is not about who would not pay the bill, but rather to attain the honor of payment. As a rather thrifty and sometimes tight-fisted German, I had learned how to think differently. However, it was very difficult to "win" against Necati. Either he had paid before I ever noticed, or he was more obstinate and thus stronger than I in the skirmish at the cash register: "No way, you're our guests! There's no way I'm going to let this happen! I have change!"

Hospitality also goes together with generosity. Whenever we visited Necati and Semse, he would excitedly take on the role of the Turkish head of the household—to entertain his guests, to keep them happy and make their visit as pleasant as possible with special foods, picnics with skilled grilling, and special films from the video rental store. He even felt responsible for joyful conversations at the dinner table.

Necati was not only a deep thinker and a sensitive person, but he also personified the Turkish zest for life. He could be a great joker, he loved to dance, and he enthusiastically played with his two kids.

— Necati would also be ready to go to prison and even die for the greatest Friend in his life, Jesus. —

His life proved that my brother-in-law also possessed Turkish ferventness. Faithfulness and the willingness to be sacrificial is expected of every Turk in what he would consider to be true friendship. Necati not only exhibited these qualities in his relationship to us, but he would also be ready to go to prison and even die for the greatest Friend in his life, Jesus.

A Wholehearted Muslim

NECATI SPENT his last years in high school in Rize, a province on the Black Sea in northeastern Turkey which is famous for its tea. He was in a boarding school that was financed by conservative Muslims.

In the secular state of Turkey, the education system should actually be neutral regarding religion. Boarding schools, however, are one of the institutions over which Islamic groups can still exert strong influence. The boarding school that young Necati Aydin attended was run by the Nurcular. This religious movement was started by the Turkish-Islamic thinker Bediuzzaman Said Nursi (1876–1960) and today is being led mostly by Fethullah Gülen, who lives in the U.S.

Did Necati's parents or older siblings want him to go to an Islamic school far away from the liberal western part of Turkey? Or did they see his attendance there just as a good opportunity to save on the normal school costs and thus financially alleviate their large family?

Necati as a Muslim at the ritual washing

Without a doubt his family was of a conservative Islamic background, even when seen from a Turkish perspective. One of Necati's older brothers would later become a teacher of religion at a public school. Another would become politically active in the Refah ("Prosperity") party—the forerunner of the AK ("Justice and Development") party, which is presently the ruling party. He was once a candidate for the position of precinct leader. One of Necati's half-sisters is to this day very active in calling women together for prayer and religious instruction. Her husband is an *imam* (a prayer leader and preacher) in a mosque.

Even when in primary school, Necati, like many other children in Turkey, attended Qur'an courses. There the fundamentals of the doctrines and practices of Islam are taught on weekends or during the school vacation. Pupils are taught to read the Qur'an in Arabic, without having to understand it. They learn to memorize in Arabic the most important prayers and some *surahs* (chapters) of the Qur'an. Necati would achieve the honorable title of *hatim*, which is given to those who have read the whole Qur'an aloud.

In the boarding school Necati was definitely exposed to an even more Islamic environment. Older students were assigned to the freshmen as *abis* (older brothers) for their spiritual welfare. They encouraged them to regularly pray the ritual prayers and instructed them more deeply in Islam according to the Nurcular. A peer pressure developed, which most submitted to. Necati seems to have readily accepted what he was taught about Allah and his laws. Even then he was very devoted and had a zeal to accomplish God's will and escape hell.

His religious search continued after his time on the Black Sea and his return to his parents' home in Menemen near Izmir. He passed the exam for a correspondence course in business, and he started working as a book-keeper in a company in Izmir to help support his family financially. At the time an older brother, his wife, and their six children were living with Necati's parents. The other siblings had already moved out.

Could Necati have become an extremist, a Muslim who would have been prepared to become violent? My sister-in-law Semse said later that she thought his sincerity, his natural politeness, and his love for others would have kept him from violent extremism.

In any case, Necati wanted to be as obedient as he possibly could to the God he knew up until then. He read religious-philosophy books with his religious friends, tried to understand the Qur'an better, and encouraged others to practice Islam. He wrote down notes when he performed the obligatory ritual prayers five times a day. If he missed one of the prayer times, he would try to make it up later (which is according to Islamic doctrine) so that he would not have a deficit before God. Because he had a sincere heart, he had to admit that he often did not meet the strict standard of Islamic regulations, and that he thereby also could not fulfill his own standards.

He did not have an assurance that he would go to paradise either. Devout Muslims regard such an assurance as presumptuous and a limitation on almighty God's freedom to decide to throw into hell those whom he will and to bring into paradise those whom he will. However, in spite of knowing that he had a deficit before God, Necati Aydin, like all other serious Muslims, was convinced that he belonged to the last and final religion and thereby that he was superior to people of all other faiths.

This would all change in an unexpected and surprising meeting with a Christian on a city bus in the Gaziemir section of Izmir. There he would meet Semse Kilciksiz, the sister of my wife. She would turn out to not only lead him to Jesus, but also to be his wife and the mother of his children.

A Courageous Messenger of Jesus

S EMSE'S LIFE was similar to Necati's in a way, but there were also extreme differences. Semse was born as the fourth of nine children to a road construction worker in the small Christian village of Tokacli near Antakya.

The modern Turkish Antakya is the "Syrian Antioch" of the Bible, the place where the disciples of Jesus were first called Christians (Acts 11:26) and where the missionary journeys of Paul began (Acts 13:1–3). The small Greek Orthodox minority, which has spoken Arabic for centuries, has remained there since the time of New Testament Christianity. The power of the Holy Spirit, however, does not appear to have remained with them. The daily life of many Christians there was not influenced by the Word of God. The witness of the small group of Orthodox Christians is weak. Many do not at all believe that the gospel is also valid for their Muslim neighbors. They, just like many Muslims, are convinced that one's faith passes from one generation to the next, as if it were transfused through the blood.

For Semse, whose family later moved to Izmir, this form of faith was not attractive. Early on the young woman claimed to be an atheist. She worked hard, cursed a lot, smoked like a chimney—and was fundamentally in despair. When her *abla*, her older sister, became a believer in Christ and found her spiritual home in a newly established Turkish Protestant church, Semse reacted with decisive rejection: "Leave me alone with this religious stuff!"

At some point Semse took part in a spiritist meeting, without any conviction about it, but just out of curiosity. Afterward an evil spirit began to scare her. Back then she had been working with her sister in a printer's shop making proofs. Fearful, she could no longer stay in the darkroom where the film was developed. She had the inescapable fear that a dark power was taking over.

A psychiatrist whom she saw subsequently confirmed that she was not ill. Although she did not believe either in God or in spirits, she turned to her believing sister: "I need some sort of help!"

"When this dark shadow and fear return," counseled Janet, "you turn to Jesus and command the spirit to leave you alone in the name of Jesus."

Somewhat ashamedly Semse later told her sister that she did it and it worked. She still could not accept the Christian faith, but she said, "Now I want to learn about Jesus, who has freed me."

She read the New Testament intensely and was fascinated by Jesus and His Word. With spiritual hunger and deep understanding she read the Bible. The Spirit of God fundamentally changed her life.

From the beginning of her life as a Christian, Semse was a zealous missionary. Janet, who had already been a sort of second mother to the many younger siblings in their large family, also became a spiritual mother for Semse. In a Christian student group in Izmir, Semse was trained in how to give an evangelistic testimony.

From 1993 to 1994 I was in Izmir to learn Turkish. There I got to know my then-future wife. I also met Semse there, who shared an apartment with Janet then. Life was hard for her both financially and emotionally, but she was shining for Jesus.

From the beginning of her life as a Christian, Semse was a zealous missionary.

After I returned to Germany, Janet and I experienced problems during our engagement, and Semse wrote me a couple of letters to help us. Without any deletions to these, one could use them as sermons, and this showed how filled she was with God's Word and her zeal for Jesus.

Semse's faith was influenced by her acceptance of the Bible as simple and as radical as it is. This left no room for doubt and subtleness, and sometimes not for shades of meaning either. This radical approach seemed unavoidable for her—and it would be a life-saving support for her in the hardest challenges of her life, which were yet to come.

Unconditional Love and Forgiveness

T HESE SO DIFFERENT worlds of Necati and Semse collided in November 1994. Semse was working as a secretary in a Christian travel agency, Necati as a bookkeeper in another company. Both businesses were in the Gaziemir section of the city only two or three bus stops away from each other.

One day when Necati got on the bus after work, the seat next to Semse was empty. At first he passed by. In Turkish buses one always tries to find a seat next to someone of the same gender, especially if one is a religious person. Since the seat next to Semse was the only empty one on the whole bus, Necati, tired, cautiously sat next to her.

Semse was going through notes from a Christian seminar. Consciously she held her notes a little in the direction of her neighbor. She thought that could be a good way to start an evangelistic conversation. Necati, who was curious about the religious terms he saw out of the corner of his eye, became suspicious. "Are you a missionary?" was the first question he asked Semse.

In Turkey the word "missionary" has a rather unpleasant connotation. In Islamic propaganda and in the opinion of most Turks, missionaries are the agents of enemy powers who try to undermine the country with Western thought. To call a Christian a "missionary" is almost like putting one in the same category as criminals.

Semse reacted unafraid with a counterattack: "Are you serious about your own faith? If you are, then you are also a missionary."

"You are correct," Necati had to admit.

Shortly afterward both "missionaries" found themselves in a deep discussion about the Christian faith. Semse asked Necati if he was interested in having a New Testament. He affirmed he was. Since she did not have one with her, they exchanged telephone numbers. Her cultural upbringing and also her evangelistic training had taught her that such gestures can be misunderstood by men. However, she was impressed by the honest and spiritually hungry way this young man asked questions and then listened. "Aside from that he seemed to be so harmless and innocent," remarked Semse in reflection.

Three months passed and Semse heard nothing from the young man she met on the bus. Many questions arose in Necati's mind, but it took a long time before he decided to make a call. Was it not doubt and also a sin to seriously grapple with a different faith? As a conservative Muslim he had been educated to think in this manner, and Necati wanted to avoid sin and please God! But then the questions, and his interest in the missionary, became greater than the fear of sinning by considering matters critical of Islam.

In the following months it became a custom for the two to take the same bus to the Cafe Riyo in the Kemeralti section of Izmir after work. Almost daily Necati and Semse sat there for about two hours talking about Jesus and His message as they drank tea.

Necati asked the normal questions about the Christian faith: "We also believe in the Old Testament (*Tevrat* and *Zebur*—the Law and the Psalms) and the New Testament (*Injil*), but wasn't the Bible changed later? Don't you believe in three gods? How can Jesus be God's Son? Isn't Islam as the last also the greatest of all the monotheistic religions based on a revelation? If Christians believe that Jesus died for all sins, doesn't that give them a license to sin?"

Necati studying the Bible

Semse tried to give answers using practical examples. If no more questions came, she asked her own or simply opened the New Testament and enthusiastically explained any part of the Bible. Additionally she gave the young man a New Testament and good Christian literature.

Necati became increasingly fascinated by Jesus and His message. He was especially influenced by the Sermon on the Mount. Soon afterward he also read parts of it to his mother at home. The young man had felt for a long time that he could not fulfill Islam's requirements, but he really did not have any blatant or manifest sin in his life. In the Sermon on the Mount he realized that God accounts even our evil thoughts, motivations, and the secret impulses of our inner person as sin. This truth became clear to Necati.

However, what really prepared the young Muslim to believe on Christ was the unconditional love and forgiveness that were offered him in Jesus. To be good and do God's will, that was something he wanted to do as a Muslim—but Jesus offered love to sinners. With Jesus he did not have to first improve his lifestyle in order to be accepted. Islam could never give Necati the assurance of eternal salvation. In the past he had always answered the question of assurance like every good Muslim—by saying, "*Takdir Allah'in* (That is at God's discretion)!" Now he realized that because of the unearned gift of Jesus, this assurance is possible for us. This message was an irresistible attraction to him.

Semse reflects that Necati almost never told her anything about Islam. "What could he say? Jesus was simply fascinating to him, and he quickly noticed that he could not compete with Him."

After about a year the young bookkeeper decided: he wanted to be a follower of Jesus. As a Muslim Necati had already tried to avoid sin and to please God, but now he fled into the arms of the loving God. It was as if the son was finally returning to his Father.

Two Watermelons Under One Arm

THERE IS A Turkish proverb about undecided people: "He's trying to carry two watermelons under one arm." In the years after turning to Jesus in 1995, Necati Aydin tried to perform this feat. The truth that Jesus had accepted him unconditionally was Necati's great discovery, and so it was without question for him that his life belonged to Jesus. However, he feared losing his family, who meant so much to him.

Necati already knew from reading verses from the Sermon on the Mount to his mother and father that revealing himself as a Christian would be considered a catastrophe by his family. Because of these readings and the Christian books he had, his older brother understood that Necati was seriously considering Christianity. When Necati defended Christian ideas in a discussion, the older brother put a pistol in his lap and warned him soberly, "If you continue to walk in this way, I will shoot you in the knee, so that you will not be able to walk anymore."

Necati knew all too well that if one's child converted to Christianity it would be considered a scandal even in a not-so-religious family. If a father would not resolutely prevent one's falling away from Islam, he would be viewed as a failure in society, as one who had not been able to protect his own child from such a false religion. Whoever openly rejects Islam is also seen as a traitor who has betrayed his Turkish identity. How much more extreme would the reaction of Necati's devout Islamic family be? Necati's parents and siblings sincerely believed that the acceptance of the Christian faith and the deity of Jesus is idolatry, which could only be punished by eternity in hell.

Necati regularly met with Semse in the following year. She took him to her church, which at the time was the only Turkish-speaking Protestant church in the three-million metropolis of Izmir, and introduced him to other Christians. Just like Semse, Necati loved God's Word, and in his first years as a Christian he read the Bible from cover to cover many times. In his own family, however, after the first confrontations, Necati did not give any reason for them to doubt his belief in Islam. He continued to be the obedient son and brother.

In reality, Necati was even trying to carry three watermelons under his arm. A relationship between him and Semse had developed, which involved more than just the spiritual. Necati had fallen in love with Semse earlier and Semse had been fighting with her feelings for a long time; wasn't Necati too young? How strong was his new faith?

Necati and Semse at their engagement
(according to custom, a red ribbon is cut)

Could she be his "spiritual mother" and wife at the same time?

Once she even tried to introduce Necati to a young Turkish woman, who had also come to Jesus by her witness. Fortunately the matchmaking attempt failed. Soon afterward Necati and Semse secretly gave their word to marry.

The Beginning of Love and Suffering

J ANET AND I were married in a civil ceremony in April
1995 in Izmir, then I returned to Germany. At the time
we knew nothing of the relationship between her sister
and future brother-in-law. After Janet had received her
visa, she moved to Germany in May and Semse accompanied her. Our church wedding would be that June in my
home church in Heinebach in northern Hessen.

Janet had waited impatiently for Semse to take a taxi
to the airport. Semse arrived very late, and because of this
the two were so irritated and under so much stress that
they left some important items in the taxi. At the time
Semse did not want to tell her irritated older sister that
she had been delayed by a farewell meeting with Necati.

A year later, at the end of August 1996, Necati began
his eighteen-month military service, a requirement for
all young men in Turkey. Religious books are forbidden
in the Turkish military. During his basic training in Tokat,

in central Anatolia, one of the trainers found a New Testament that Necati had smuggled in his baggage. The New Testament landed in the toilet, and as punishment the young soldier had to crawl on the hard ground with short sleeves until his arms bled.

However, there were other soldiers who had respect for God's Word. In actuality, Muslims are taught that the Old and New Testaments are also books sent down by Allah. A Muslim comrade could not accept that such a holy book should land in a toilet, and he "rescued" it for Necati.

In the military Necati experienced the beginning of his sufferings as a Christian. At the same time, however, he learned the value of Christian fellowship. After finishing his basic training, he was stationed in northern Cyprus. There he had contact with an English couple who had faithfully led a small Turkish Christian fellowship for years. On his free weekends he experienced their Christian family life and learned a lot about what it means to follow Jesus Christ.

Necati as a soldier

Necati also experienced his first tangible miracle as a soldier. In the arid and hot northern part of Cyprus, water is sometimes in short supply, and if one cannot shower, he is more vulnerable to small bugs. So lice were a widespread problem for the soldiers, who were constantly itching and scratching themselves. In one of his occasional telephone conversations with Semse, Necati complained about this problem.

Semse recommended to her fiancé: "In Egypt the people of God were exempted from the plagues that the Egyptians suffered. Command the lice in Jesus' name to go away from you."

Due to his constant scratching the desperate Necati tried it out and later reported enthusiastically by phone to Semse: "It worked! After I prayed the lice really jumped off of me. Now all of my roommates are still complaining about the plague, but there is not a single louse on my skin."

After completing his military service, Necati received an honorable discharge with the remark "great success." According to the judgment of his commanders he was considered to be "trustworthy and faithful...sincere, diligent, and respectful." After Necati's death, Semse used this evaluation in some interviews to show how wrong it is to think that Christians cannot be good Turks. "Necati served his country wholeheartedly and was expressly praised for this." Since military service in Turkey is not well paid and one receives little vacation time, marriages are usually postponed until afterward. When Necati returned to Izmir at the beginning of March 1998, the young pair decided to make their engagement public.

Necati told his parents that he wanted to marry Semse, a Christian woman. At the same time he let his beloved family know, for the first time, that he himself—their son, brother, and uncle—had given his life to Jesus Christ.

Semse first got the carrot, and later the stick. Unexpectedly, she received a call from one of Necati's older brothers: "We are calling you because of a joyous occasion" —this is generally said before weddings. "Our brother has told us that he wants to marry you, and we welcome you into our family—but on one condition: you must become a Muslima!"

As had become typical for Semse since she had trusted Jesus, she reacted very clearly and radically to even the

— "We welcome you into our family—but on one condition: you must become a Muslima!" —

most subtle invitation to compromise in matters of faith. For her, to play for time or try to find middle ground in such a moment of decision was not an option. "It is completely out of the question for me to become a Muslima," she stated firmly. "I have not planned to marry Necati as a Muslim. The Necati I want to marry is a Christian."

Serious Crises and the Final Decision

AFTER WE MET Necati personally in the summer of 1996, we followed the relationship of the two with some reservations. Was Necati really the right man for Janet's sister?

We did not see Necati again until after their marriage. For various reasons we were not able to go to Turkey in 1997 and 1998. Following this, however, the two sisters phoned each other numerous times. According to Turkish culture the *abla*, the older sister, is allowed to meddle in family matters, and the younger sister knew that Janet really wanted the best for her. In any event, we prayed from Germany for God's clear leading for both of them.

Soon after the end of Necati's military service we received a shocking call from Semse: "It's all over! I have spoken to Necati and he told me that he is and will remain a Muslim." For her that meant: "If God doesn't bring him back, then it's over for me."

Again, Semse's clear, unwavering stand was a key to later "success." To marry Necati under these so different circumstances was out of the question.

Had God in this manner shown that He did not want this relationship? This thought crossed our minds, but we continued to pray. Today, in retrospect, we see that this crisis offered Necati the opportunity to make a more radical decision to devote himself to Christ.

Later we learned that he was sent to his brother who taught religion in Bartin in the Black Sea region. If nothing else, Necati had backed off because of the threats his family had made toward Semse. However, in the home of his brother he fell into deep depression. He did not eat and cried constantly. After he had apparently decided for his family and against Jesus and Semse, he realized that his life would end in spiritual death, if he left his source of life. After about ten days his condition became so desperate that his brother finally threw him out. "Do what you want," his brother said, "but you no longer belong to us. You have betrayed us and our faith!"

Semse told us later that in this tense time of waiting she prayed, "Lord Jesus, bring him back, not for me, but for you!" When Semse went to the bus stop one morning, Necati was waiting for her. She exploded with joy. However, at the same time it was a step of faith for her to begin again under such dramatic circumstances.

It could be a trick—he could just be acting. Maybe his family had married him off in the meantime and was trying to draw me away from my faith, she thought.

She soon noticed that Necati had now made a clear decision—for Jesus Christ, for the relationship with Semse, and against the pressure of his family. Necati was temporarily able to stay with another bachelor from the small church in Izmir. The preparations for their wedding were begun.

For Necati's large family, the youngest son was considered an infidel from that point on. One of the older sisters called Semse one day and said bitterly, "You've won!"

Semse answered, "Not I, but the Lord, who is truth, has won."

The relatives saw Necati as a traitor, as a blemish on the family. For years he and Semse later tried to build bridges on a purely human basis, so that the relationship would not totally break down. Some Turkish families calm down when the first children are born to a rejected couple. Later Necati and Semse intentionally let Necati's parents and siblings see their children.

Despite his humility and his willingness to help in any emergency, Necati always got the cold shoulder from almost all of his relatives and was confronted with new accusations again and again. Certainly they all loved Necati, but they simply could not live with the fact that he had become an "apostate" and had left "the highest and best religion." After Necati's death we found a photo of young Necati as he was standing on the pulpit of a mosque reading the Qur'an. On the back of the picture probably a brother or sister noted the bitter comment: "I guess now you live out the religion of the idolaters with a cross around your neck and became a priest."

When Necati's father died in 1999, Necati was informed a few days afterward—an unimaginable and serious affront against one's own brother in Turkish culture. Necati's beloved mother died in 2006. He knew that she had been ill for a long time, and was able to visit her again

Necati as a young man reading the Qur'an on the pulpit of a mosque

for a few days. But as with his father's death, he learned of her death too late to arrive in time for the burial.

At some point after that Necati confessed that he did not have much hope left that the relationships in his family would improve. He loved his family, but he no longer had the strength to always reach out to them, only to be rejected.

After Necati's death, one of his brothers gave the press one of Necati's personal letters. Even Semse read the letter for the first time in the local Malatya newspaper. The brother wanted to show that Necati's Christian faith had caused his separation from the family. If one really knows the background and about Necati's continual attempts to build bridges, this letter is a great testimony of a son who loved, but who found his greatest love in Jesus.

Necati's life demonstrates in a very practical way how Jesus expects a clear decision from His followers: "He who loves father or mother more than Me is not worthy of Me. And he who loves son or daughter more than Me is not worthy of Me. And he who does not take up his cross and follow after Me is not worthy of Me" (Matthew 10:37,38).

My beloved mom, my beloved dad,
my beloved brothers and sisters,

First of all, I greet and kiss you in the exalted name of the Lord Jesus Christ. After so much confusion and conflict I have decided to live separated from you so that I may retain and live out my faith in Jesus Christ and keep this truth till the end. This decision was not made based on fear or on anything that I longed for or demanded, but was made after much conflict in myself. Therefore accuse no one else. Do not wear yourselves out by thinking about all of the possible theories. I have returned to where I belong. I have returned to Jesus and the fellowship of His church.

Just as you are my physical family, I also have a family in the Spirit. Do not be afraid or worried about my separation from you! Do not be sad and do not be depressed! For I have not been saved to lose something, but rather to gain something eternally. Therefore rejoice! I have gained this salvation through my faith in Jesus. Neither poverty, nor difficulty, neither illness, nor evil, neither death, nor a person can turn me away from this saving faith. The power I have to live and be saved —my spiritual arteries, so to speak—are bound to Jesus in faith. To live without Him means to deserve death and eternal separation.

From now on in our relationship I will love you, remain in contact with you, and pray for you, that you may also be saved. However, I do not want you to call us at the moment or contact us in another manner, but rather that you be patient and wait a little, to extinguish the feelings of your hatred, that you may plant love, tenderness, and understanding in its place, and most of all that you meet Jesus Christ, who is the "truth, way and life," that you believe on Him and thus gain eternal life.

I love you. May the Lord let you encounter His truth. Amen!

Rana Necati Aydin

Even after Necati's murder we have been unable to notice any softer attitude among his relatives. One day after the terrible murders we were sitting in his apartment with Semse and other Christians when the doorbell rang. It was Necati's oldest brother.

In all of the sadness, Semse responded surprised and even joyful. Could it be that God was using the death of her husband to bring his family closer? After a short talk over a glass of hot tea came the rude awakening: The family had not sent the oldest to express their condolences, but his main purpose was to demand the corpse of his brother to bury him according to Islamic rite. Semse, of course, rejected his demand.

Two days later at Necati's Christian burial held in Izmir, not far from his home in Menemen, not one of Necati's brothers or sisters was present. We continue to pray for them.

"Heavenly Father, Plan Our Wedding!"

IT HAD BECOME clear to Necati and Semse that they wanted to marry as soon as possible. But how could they afford it? Both were unemployed at the time. In Turkish culture, the families of the bride and groom pay for the furnishing of the first apartment and the planning of the wedding according to a pretty set tradition. However, Necati's family was radically against this marriage and Semse didn't have many relatives who could help them.

The couple decided not to beg for help from people. They sat down at a table and prayed: "Dear Father in heaven, since we can expect no help from our earthly fathers, please plan our wedding."

Surprisingly, Necati's Christian acquaintances from his military service in Cyprus asked about how they could help. Then, without knowing the exact need, the small fellowship there collected precisely the amount that Necati and Semse had previously estimated to be the minimum amount they would need. This provision was a great encouragement to believe that God would also care for them as a Father in the future.

After a simple but beautiful wedding in the Izmir Karatash church on May 7, 1998, the two started their marriage, poor but as happy as children. During the first three months they had to live from the financial gifts from the wedding. Then Necati found a job as a book-keeper at a factory that produced *lokum*—"Turkish delight" (sweet candy).

In numerous later situations they experienced God's help in a practical way. That was also the case as the family grew. In July 2000 Elisa Günes was born. "Elisa" is the name of the Old Testament prophet Elisha in Turkish. Almost exactly a year later the small Ester (Esther) Bahar followed her older brother.

Necati and Semse's wedding in May 1998

A New Family

WHEN OUR DAUGHTER Debora was ten months old, we asked Necati and Semse to be her Turkish guardians. We wanted to have her blessed in Janet's home church, the Izmir Karatash church, so we flew to Turkey for a vacation in May 1999, our first trip in a couple of years. We stayed with Necati and Semse most of the time in the Osmangazi section of Izmir.

It was then that we learned about Necati's hospitality. He was still pretty much a stranger to us then, but he really tried to make our vacation as enjoyable as possible, despite his limitations with respect to time and money. Evenings he brought us candy from his company, and he even knew someone who offered us a week in his cottage by the seaside. During this vacation our relationship with our dear Turkish brother-in-law began to grow. The small apartment became our address for visits in Turkey, and our vacations in the years that followed strengthened and deepened this relationship.

Necati and Semse radiated joy about how they could now openly serve their Lord Jesus Christ together. In their church they led a home group meeting with much devotion. Necati became one of the driving forces in the Karatash church. His pastor, Zekai Tanyar, who is from an Islamic background and a very sincere person, felt especially close to Necati. After Necati's death, Zekai wrote:

> Necati accepted Jesus, was baptized, was married, committed his children to the Lord and served in the church he was a member of. He was meek and very serious when it came to his faith. But when I say "serious," I do not mean "religious somberness" as many might suppose. He was a good-natured and happy person.

For the next five years the church in Izmir would be home for Necati's family, and the young married couple would become a family for others. Usually the home group meetings took place in their small apartment. Mostly young people attended, either those who had recently trusted in Christ or who were still seekers.

Although Necati himself was young in the Christian faith, he very quickly became a big brother and even a spiritual father to other young men. He was serious about what he believed. Because of his own need to be so, however, he had a very holistic approach with his "spiritual disciples," engaging with them not just in Bible study but in other life activities. To drink tea together was a fundamental practice for human fellowship in Turkey anyway, but Necati was also the initiator for soccer games or evening bowling. Often home group members came for a meal and afterward board games were brought to the table. Necati and Semse studied the Bible with their friends in this personal setting, and Necati led numerous young men through discipleship classes.

After Necati's murder, when we were in Izmir for the burial and then attended the Sunday service in his home church, we met some young men who, with tears in their eyes, reported what a role Necati had played in their lives as Christians. Especially moving was that one of these young Turks with whom Necati had read the Bible and played soccer years earlier, stood in front of the Karatash church and moderated the service with an impressive spiritual zeal.

Since the support of family was lacking, Necati and Semse became even more dedicated to their fellowship, and this included, for example, the cleaning of the toilets in the church building. They were also involved in an interdenominational student ministry, and when a new church was opened in the Bornova section of Izmir they tried to attend the Sunday afternoon worship services there. The leaders of the new church were foreigners and appreciated having Turkish disciples of Jesus there.

Only a few months after the wedding, Necati found an opportunity to be baptized. During a conference of his church at a Christian retreat center very near ancient Ephesus, he was baptized in the name of Jesus Christ in a small outdoor pool.

Because of their different culture, it is probably difficult for Christians in the West to understand the importance of Christian baptism for people from an Islamic background. Baptism is a very apparent and tangible finalization of the old life without Jesus. It is also a clear break from all connections to the former faith. In many cities

Necati's baptism, summer 1998

of Turkey without a Christian church, believers can only be baptized in secret, or they must travel to a different city. It is a real celebration for the small churches to be able to have public baptisms in their places of worship or in lakes or in the sea.

Necati had already made the decision to leave his old life behind. Nevertheless, the public proclamation of this decision in baptism was a great joy for him and Semse. Perhaps the verse Semse chose for him at his baptism was in his thoughts when he was in prison later or even as the murderers attacked him with a knife later still. In John 10:28 Jesus promises His "sheep," those who follow Him: "I give them eternal life, and they shall never perish; neither shall anyone snatch them out of My hand."

On the Stage of Life

A FTER ABOUT A year of married life, Necati had the opportunity to serve his Lord more publicly. A Turkish Christian publishing house asked Necati to work for them. Zirve Publishing publishes and distributes the New Testament and Christian literature as well as the Turkish version of the popular *JESUS* film, which portrays the life of Jesus Christ according to the Gospel of Luke.

Necati and Semse had not looked for such a job. But when this opportunity was laid at their feet, they accepted it enthusiastically. Their entire lives were directed toward spreading the good news about Jesus anyway. Necati saw this as a God-given opportunity to be able to do this as a job, and he gladly accepted it.

In February 1999 Christian churches in Izmir were planning a large evangelistic project: to take lay actors with professional qualities from the churches and perform the life of Jesus as a public drama. The organizers asked Necati to play the main role of Jesus.

With Zirve Publishing House at a Book Fair

Rehearsals and performances lasted about two years. The drama was performed in Turkey's three largest cities: Izmir (Christmas 1999), Ankara (Easter 2000), and Istanbul (Easter 2001). About 2,500 people, many of them not Christian, came out to see the largest performance in the convention center in Istanbul's Bostanci section. A video recording was made of one of the performances and was later distributed as a CD.

Semse also played in the Christmas 1999 performance of "The Life of Jesus" in the Efes Hotel in Izmir. She played, very fittingly, one of the women who went to Jesus' tomb on Easter morning. For the Easter 2000 performance in Ankara, she was too far along in her first pregnancy to play a role.

It was no mistake having given Necati the main role. He identified with the role of Jesus so credibly that his performance was the most impressive part of the drama.

Necati as "Jesus" in a drama about the life of Christ

Necati was sincere, and he wanted to follow Jesus with his whole heart. His wife said later that his portrayal of Jesus helped him to grow in his relationship to Jesus and to become more like Him—not only on the stage, but also in everyday life.

Looking back, it almost seemed prophetic that Necati had been chosen to play this role. In the drama, he carried the cross, collapsed under it, and then obediently went on. The real Necati Aydin, who followed Jesus, was not only ready to be near Jesus in times of service but also identified himself as His follower despite the rejection of his own family, despite imprisonment, and despite his brutal murder in his office in Malatya.

Today when people in Turkey view this drama CD, what they see is not professional acting, but everyone who knows what later happened to the actor playing Jesus probably gets more than goose-bumps, because in this case there is not a big gap between film and reality. Watching Necati's performance, people are touched by something genuine.

On August 17, 1999, a major disaster struck Izmit and the entire region around the Sea of Mamara in northwestern Turkey. An earthquake measuring 7.8 on the Richter scale killed 18,000 people and injured another 44,000, according to official statistics. The catastrophe in Turkey evoked aid from all over the world. Many Christians, churches, and denominations also wanted to help and looked for partners in Turkey so that the aid could be distributed in a trustworthy and effective manner. The small Protestant Christian community was faced with a great challenge.

— Necati identified himself as His follower despite the rejection of his own family, despite imprisonment, and despite his brutal murder. —

After the earthquake many foreign Christians living in Turkey and national believers were constantly busy distributing aid, looking after projects, and helping suffering people on a very personal level. This action actually overwhelmed the capacity and maturity of the believing Turkish church, which was still so weak. Many Christians, however, were enthusiastic about the possibility of finally being able to demonstrate to the Turkish people in a practical way: "We as Christians love you! We are very interested in your welfare. Despite the propaganda which tries to talk you into it, we are not the enemies of Turkey."

Even Christians were not always perfectly organized in earthquake relief and made mistakes. The reactions to the aid were divided. Newspapers tried to defame the earthquake relief as disguised propaganda for Christianity. Thousands of Muslims, however, will surely not forget that during a dark time in their country and in their lives, Christians responded quickly to help them.

Necati's new employer sent him to the north into the earthquake region, and Semse accompanied him as a volunteer helper. For several weeks the young married couple was fully involved in the relief project in Gölcük, a city that had been severely damaged about 20 kilometers (12 miles) from Izmit. They cleaned toilets in the container camps for those who had lost their houses. Under medical supervision they took the blood pressures of traumatized people and bandaged their wounds. Food aid was distributed in villages whose normal means of supply were disrupted. In this manner Necati and Semse were sharing the love of God with joy and devotion.

Thirty Days in Prison

DURING THIS TIME Janet and I were working in a church organization in Germany which presents the gospel to foreigners there. In a different way we were also trying to help the relief efforts in the area of the earthquake. We informed churches so that Christians could give money to help the victims of the earthquake, and we would then transfer these funds to aid organizations in Turkey. We were also influenced by the enthusiasm of showing practical love to the country we had a burden for.

However, a phone call from Semse changed our agenda. On September 12, 1999, she said nervously, "Janet, our whole church in Izmir has been arrested!"

We could not believe what we had heard. As Necati and Semse and some other members of the Karatash church in Izmir were distributing food a seven-hour bus ride away in Gölcük, the police came into the Sunday morning worship service of the church with a TV film crew and arrested most of those who had gathered, loaded them into cars, and took them to the local police station. A couple of young women were left behind to look after the kids.

How could this happen? Up until the end of the 1980s, Christians from the newly established Protestant churches were arrested just because they had assembled for worship services. Since then they have gotten a little more freedom. The constitution of Turkey has always guaranteed religious freedom, and a decision of the highest appeals court in 1985 expressly defined the freedom of religion as encompassing the right of assembly and the right of propagating one's own faith. Just how one forms a church, or how and where one can assemble, or which types of permits are required—on these points no laws or legal conditions had been made, and this has always lead to the disruption of young churches.

Since 1994 the believers in the Karatash church in Izmir had been meeting in the two lowest floors (which they had purchased) of a building that was mostly residential. A few weeks before the arrests, the police, who had known about the worship services for years and had been officially informed, claimed that the meeting place had not been approved by the government. All the other tenants in the building had to sign an agreement that would allow the church to hold meetings in the building. Because of group pressure in Turkish society, this is very difficult to obtain. Although the church had opened a case in an administrative court to clarify this demand, the police intervened suddenly.

Actually, the believers all over Turkey at that time knew this was an official reaction against the positive response Christians had received because of the earthquake relief. Christians also knew that in reality spiritual powers were behind the human attacks. In Germany we prayed, called on friends to pray, and tried to inform the public.

After being held an entire day at the police station, the members of the church were released. The legal wrangling afterward lasted for months. The meeting place was temporarily closed by the authorities. The Karatash believers were able to find refuge in another fellowship in Izmir until they were allowed to meet again in their own building, where they still meet today.

The believers were not mistreated at the police station —but whoever is shown on TV as a believer or even a spiritual seeker visiting a Christian worship service, and then as a prisoner at a police station, could lose his job or be ostracized by his relatives.

Necati and Semse had already dispensed with such fears. Instead, they were sad that they had not been there that Sunday in the worship service and then later in prison. In their hearts they thought, *Our church family has experienced something bad when we were away*. They would have gladly suffered with them in solidarity. They understood that it is an honor to suffer for Christ.

Soon afterward Necati had the opportunity to experience this honor personally. At the beginning of March 2000 Semse called us again: "Necati is in prison!"

Necati and Ercan (Erjan), a coworker at Zirve Publishing, had offered people New Testaments and Christian literature in a small village near Izmir. As was usual, some accepted the literature thankfully and others rejected it or glared at them angrily. When they traveled further, the two believers were arrested by the gendarmerie (Turkish military units that police the countryside) in the town of Kemalpasha and put in jail there.

Necati had been traveling for his new employer for some months. In the Aegean region of Turkey, he and Ercan had been in numerous cities, towns, and villages and had offered the resources of the publishing house to bookstores and to people who were interested. They spoke to many people, left New Testaments and *JESUS* films for them, and followed up on those who had shown an interest in the Christian faith. All of this is not liked by many Turks, but it is all perfectly legal.

Necati's arrest for distributing New Testaments

In the province of Kemalpasha the gendarmerie pressured the villagers to accuse Necati and Ercan of illegal acts. They gave affidavits: "The men forced us to accept Bibles! They insulted and cursed Islam."

In the end Necati and Ercan were charged with "sedition and breach of the peace" based on their "insulting Islam and distribution of the New Testament." Even if the accusations had been valid, holding the men in custody until the trial was totally incommensurate with the crime. This whole case should be seen as having been an attempt at intimidation.

From distant Germany I again admired Semse's great strength in crisis situations. My sister-in-law does not always find it easy to cope with the small problems in everyday life, but in great challenges her radical faith proves to be authentic. At that time her situation was not at all easy. She was five months pregnant and did not know what the outcome of the trial would be. Semse thought about all the wrongs and injustices that she had ever heard or read about. Even for people who are innocent, trials in Turkey can mean long incarcerations for those charged.

Semse was encouraged by her first visit to the prison in Kemalpasha. Necati was full of joy and zeal. "Next time bring me my Bible and my *saz* [a sort of Turkish guitar]," he requested.

Necati related that in the beginning he tried to hide his faith. In the large Turkish prison cells there are often eight to ten men and the prisoners are not well protected from one another. Necati was afraid of the prospect that a violent inmate would let out his pent-up rage at a "missionary and an apostate from Islam." Therefore, he was very cautious at first.

"Aren't you that person on TV?" called out some of the inmates.

A TV channel reported about his arrest, but the hard men reacted differently than was feared. Necati was well respected by the other inmates. Many used the opportunity to ask someone who was "in the same boat" with them about Christianity. Necati was happy to tell them why he had become a Christian, and during his imprisonment he also organized soccer games and other free-time activities.

When he left the prison thirty days later, he had gotten to know many men and some remained friends even after prison. One fellow prisoner later came to church. Necati donated his New Testament to the prison library.

However, in the beginning Necati and Semse did not yet know about how well this would turn out. The Izmir church met repeatedly to fast and pray for their two imprisoned members. Finally the day of the trial came at the court in Kemalpasha. All the believers who had prayed experienced the wonderful intervention of God in the proceedings. All the villagers whose testimony had brought the Christians into prison withdraw their testimonies! They then testified that the men from the gendarmerie had pressured them to give the false testimonies.

Because of the precedence of this case, Necati later opened and won a case against the state with legal support from the churches. He was even granted a redress, although a small one.

Semse, who had visited him three times during his month in prison, was now able to welcome him to his own apartment. The joy was great. Soberly both came to the realization that another decision lay ahead. They had personally experienced what following Jesus could cost, especially serving Him full-time in evangelism. They sat together and evaluated their situation realistically. Semse told her husband, "Necati, do not do it just to earn a living. You can earn money elsewhere."

At the time neither of them thought about death, but rather about new arrests and legal problems. Necati loved working for Jesus, and both of them, aware of the possible consequences, agreed that he would continue to go to villages and cities and tell people about Jesus.

Both of them, aware of the possible consequences, agreed that he would continue to tell people about Jesus.

Necati later wrote a song about what drove him on to tell his people about Jesus. Music was important for Necati. His beautiful and full voice carried many of the worship times in meetings.

You were in the highest of heights, but became the lowest.
You were almighty, but became the most oppressed.
You had everything, but wanted nothing.
You were everything in everybody, but remained alone and
  abandoned.

I could not understand it, I could not believe it.
I could not believe or understand it at all.

You were the merciful hand of God stretched out to us.
No one had sympathy, You were pierced by nails.
How gentle You are, You said, "Father, forgive!"
How gentle You are, You said, "Father, forgive!"

I could not understand it, I could not believe it.
I could not believe or understand it at all.

The burden of my sin was on my back, I lived under it.
I heard a voice in the distance, soft and tired also:
"Come," it said, "give Me your burden. I will carry it also."
"Come," it said, "give Me your burden. I will carry it also."

I could not understand it, I could not believe it.
I could not believe or understand it at all.

Now the Lord carries my burden, and I live free.
The impossible, which I did not know, I understand now.
Lord, without You I cannot live, I worship You.
Lord, without You I cannot live, I worship You.

I understand, I understand,
I have believed, I have believed.
I have really understood,
I believe from my heart.

Moving Into an Unfamiliar Region

IN NOVEMBER 2001, Janet and I moved to Turkey to help plant a church in Izmit, an industrial city on the east side of Istanbul. We had hardly arrived and had not even found a place to live, when Necati and Semse got on a bus with their two small children, made the seven-hour trip from Izmir to Izmit, and stayed with us for a couple of days with some English friends—just to welcome us to Turkey.

We went to visit them a few weeks later in Izmir. Our relationship with Necati and Semse became more intense as numerous visits followed. They were our only relatives in Turkey who were following Jesus and wanting to serve Him.

Then Semse went through a challenging time. The birth of her son Elisa was complicated and he was a difficult baby. Just a year later Ester was born. Growing into the role of parents of two small children demanded something from both sides. Semse was not able to help out as much as she wanted to in the ministry with Necati.

In the meantime Necati increased in his ministry and responsibility. Training sessions at Zirve Publishing helped to stabilize his foundation in his ministry and his life with Christ even more. When he visited us in Izmit we encouraged him to preach in our small church. Necati was not a brilliant speaker, but especially those in our church who had come from a Muslim background were touched by his genuineness and credibility.

There are about three thousand believers from a Muslim background—a very small number considering Turkey's population of almost 75 million.

During his travels to various places in western Turkey, Necati also visited Christians who lived in the many Turkish localities where there were no Christian churches whatsoever. It is estimated that in recent decades about one hundred small evangelical Turkish churches have formed. Many of them are so small that they should perhaps be considered to be home group meetings. In all there are about three thousand believers from a Muslim background among these—a very small number considering Turkey's population of almost 75 million. In addition, churches are very unevenly distributed over the country. About half of the one hundred churches can be found in Istanbul, Ankara, or Izmir, the three largest cities in the country. Thus in many of the eighty-one provinces, there are no Christian churches at all.

Many of the people whom Necati visited came to faith in Jesus through a Bible correspondence course, which was advertised from Istanbul in some of the large Turkish newspapers. At present more and more Turkish religious inquirers have been using the Internet to receive information and download Bible study materials. Whenever Necati or other Christian publishing house workers were in the area of such people, they tried to visit them.

In the western province of Kütahya, Necati met a young woman who had trusted Jesus as her Savior as a result of participating in a Bible correspondence course. In follow-up visits by Necati and sometimes with Semse, a friend of this sister and her mother came to faith in Christ. They began reading the Bible and praying together.

Sometime in the course of 2002, Necati and Semse began to have a personal burden for these scattered believers. "Shouldn't we move to a city where there is no Christian church? There believers have no pastoral care and inquirers have no chance to personally ask committed Christians. Maybe we should live in Kütahya?"

Actually the young family was doing well in Izmir, a city of millions. A number of small evangelical churches had formed. The Aydin family lived in a network of foreign and Turkish believers. Necati's ministry in Zirve Publishing and in the fellowship was respected. In the big city of Izmir, which is also considered to be open to the world, Christians can move about more freely and the educational possibilities for children are better than in other places in Turkey. There were many reasons for them to stay right where they were.

However, throughout 2002 Necati and Semse prayed for Kütahya and shared their thoughts about this with us. They did not want to go the more comfortable way, but wanted to devote their lives for those who had not yet heard of Christ.

At the beginning of 2003, Zirve Publishing decided that they wanted to expand their work in Turkey. Necati's employers shared the vision to reach people in other regions of Turkey, but they wanted to move out further and had the east of the country in mind. When Necati heard of the plans of his leaders, these thoughts fitted with what he and his wife had been considering. He volunteered to move to the east with his family.

He did not have much competition from his colleagues for the position: Turks from western Turkey can have culture shock when they move to the east, which is much less developed. The mentality of the partially Kurdish population is vastly different from that of western Turks, and the unfortunately frequent outbreaks of violence between Kurds and Turks still occur.

Necati was prepared to give up his fixation on Kütahya. I believe he understood that God's leading often comes together in our thoughts directed by the Holy Spirit, in situations that God has organized, and through the counsel of other people. The leadership of Zirve saw three possible "centers" for the expansion of their work: Trabzon, Van, and Malatya. Trabzon is the main city for the eastern coast of the Black Sea. The province of Van, far in the east, borders Iran. Malatya, however, is known as the gate to the east, a large city from which many other provinces in the eastern and southeastern parts of the country can be relatively easily reached.

Necati and Semse could imagine living in any of the three areas. They simply knew that they wanted to reach people with the gospel of Christ—where was not so important. They began praying for the "right" city in the east.

In early 2003 we traveled from Izmit to Izmir to attend a conference there. Of course we stayed with the Aydins. Shortly before, we had heard that Malatya was one of the new ministry alternatives for our relatives. It worked out well that I was able to meet a South African Christian at the conference. He and his family were also considering moving from Mersin to Malatya. I introduced him to Necati. Perhaps God was using that as yet another piece of the puzzle in His leading. They conversed with each other, but at that point nothing concrete developed.

In the summer Necati and Semse finally had the opportunity to take a trip to the east. They made a detour to Izmit, so that we could look after their children while they were gone. We took Necati and Semse to the bus

The couples Aydin and Haede

The Republic of Turkey (Türkiye Cumhuriyeti)

Founding: October 29, 1923, by Mustafa Kemal (later called Atatürk) as succession state of the Ottoman Empire, which was divided following World War I.

Surface: approx. 780,000 square km (302,000 square miles).

Population: approx. 75,000,000. Capital: Ankara (4,400,000). Other large cities: Istanbul (13,200,000), Izmir (3,350,000), Bursa (1,900,000). More than 25% of the population is under age 14.

Biblical Places: In today's Turkey there are a lot of places mentioned in the New Testament, such as Antioch (Antakya), Tarsus, Troas, Lystra, Derbe, and all seven locations of the churches mentioned in Revelation 2 and 3.

GEORGIA

• Trabzon

Erzurum

• Hinis

Kayseri

• Malatya

Van

KEY

Antakya

SYRIA

IRAQ

Religions: Officially more than 99% of the population are Muslims, less than 0.15% Christian (approx. 100,000), and less than 0.04% Jews (23,000).

Christian Churches: Armenian-Apostolic Church (60,000), Greek-Orthodox Church (3,500), Catholic Church (21,000 in different rites). Beside three Armenian-Protestant churches in Istanbul and a few churches for foreign Protestants, during the last decades small Turkish-Protestant churches came into existence, consisting mostly of converts from Muslim background. The total number of Christians in these churches is slightly more than 3,000.

Sources: www.allaboutturkey.com/info.htm, Wikipedia article "Turkey."

Necati and Semse Aydin with Ester Bahar and Elisa Günes (in 2002)

that was headed for Malatya. In Turkey people are used to long bus rides. The ride to Malatya, with short stops, takes about fourteen hours. They wanted to see Malatya and then travel on to Van. They thought they could visit Trabzon later.

After some days we received a short call. "We will be coming back a little later!"

"They're just using their time to be able to do something without the kids," we commented with a smile.

A few days later, when we picked up Necati and Semse from the bus station, they looked younger and like a couple who had just fallen in love, and we still thought: "That was really good for them."

However, it was not first and foremost because they had been together as a couple. Our friends had come to an inner calm concerning God's leading. That inner calm had worked its way through to their outward appearance; in spite of the long journey, they appeared to be physically refreshed.

As soon as they had arrived in Malatya, they felt, *This is it. This is the right place for us.* Later they said, "We had peace about it!"

They really could not give any other explanation. The city is nice. If you travel down the road from Kayseri to Malatya in the spring or summer, one notices the expansive green apricot orchards. However, Malatya cannot even compare to Izmir, the pearl of the Aegean. In the further surroundings of Malatya are mostly long-barren, deforested mountains. But Necati and Semse felt deep down in their hearts, *This is the city where God wants to have us.* They saw no need to travel to the other possibilities.

The assurance of being led by God did not leave Necati and Semse, even after Necati's death. Even today Semse says, "I do not regret it that we went to Malatya then."

In autumn Necati traveled alone once again to the apricot city, to find an appropriate place to live. It proved to be difficult. He did not find anything to meet their expectations. The bus ticket for the return trip to Izmir had already been bought, but Necati made a spontaneous decision to delay his return by one day. Then he found a very convenient apartment for his family which would also be large enough to have visitors experience God's love there. The bus that Necati originally wanted to return on had an accident that night in which a passenger died. In retrospect Semse said, "Our Lord did not want my husband to die in such a meaningless way."

Ugur's Great Love

I N THE LATTER half of 2002, a young construction tech-
nology student from the University of Kocaeli showed
up at our church in Izmit.

He came from Elazig, a city neighboring Malatya. He
was from a family rooted in Aleviism, a special group in
Islam, which because of their more liberal lifestyle, is
despised by many Muslim hardliners. In Izmit an apartment container left over from the time of the earthquake
there served as his dorm.

He was Ugur Yüksel, who had given his life to Jesus
Christ not long before that. Far away from his home and
family, he had a lot of time alone to think about God. He
had received a New Testament from an Internet address.
As soon as he started to read it, it became clear to him:
"The God I have been looking for all of my life is talking
to me!" Within a week he had read through the whole
New Testament many times. He was also especially impressed by the Sermon on the Mount. Within a very short

time he decided to serve Jesus Christ. This decision bound him to Jesus and he would hold fast to Him through his suffering and death.

I met Ugur a little later and he seemed to be shy, somewhat self-conscious but a decidedly faithful person. Shortly before he found Jesus, he had told a friend, "A person must die either for something good or for his great love." Later he would die together with Necati and Tilmann for both something good and his great love—his love for Jesus.

As soon as he started to read it, it became clear to him: "The God I have been looking for all of my life is talking to me!"

Ugur started searching and met a Christian from Istanbul, a neighboring metropolis. He prayed together with him "officially" to invite Jesus into his life. The Turkish brother sent him to our small church in Izmit.

He would sit on the edge of the sofa when we held our Bible studies, and was usually quiet but very attentive. When he spoke, one noticed the fire in him—the fire of unused devotion which one often sees in eastern Turkey—and the fire of his love for Jesus.

After a few months Ugur had to discontinue his education. His parents no longer had the financial means to support him. Our newly won brother returned to his home in Elazig. There he tried to open a small telephone store. For almost a year he was without fellowship as a Christian. There was no Christian church anywhere near

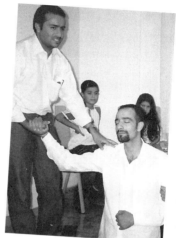

Ugur Yüksel

Necati at Ugur's baptism

him, not even a group of Christians who met to pray or read the Bible. Ugur lived from his personal relationship with Christ, and from telephone conversations with me or other Christians from Istanbul.

Representative of his attitude was something I remember from a telephone conversation: "Wolfgang, I have read that Christians give their tithes [that is, ten percent of their income] to God. How can I send money to the church in Izmit?"

I was very touched. Often people came into our fellowship asking for money, because they had read the lies of the media: Christians buy the souls of Muslims with dollars. However, Ugur did not want to receive, but to give, because Jesus had made him inwardly wealthy.

When it became clear that Necati and Semse were going to move to Malatya, I gave them Ugur's contact information. Necati was very responsible in such matters. He began phoning Ugur even before the move. The contact eventually grew between Elazig and Malatya, which was about ninety minutes away by car, and developed into a deep friendship. Later, from time to time, Christians and those showing an interest in Jesus in Elazig met for Bible studies.

During a visit with the Aydins in Malatya, we also spent some time with Ugur in Elazig. His business did not go well. Due to lack of finances he was still unable to marry his long-time girlfriend. Nevertheless, his decision for Jesus was irrevocable.

Especially in eastern Turkish culture male friendship plays an important role. One can expect everything of a *dost*, a genuine friend. He must always be available to help and especially in a time of need he must prove his faithfulness. One must also be prepared to give everything he has for his *dost*. Ugur had found his *dost* in Jesus.

Like many other Turks, Ugur also expressed his feelings in poetry. One of his poems gives a deep insight into his stance in the faith:

Here I Am

We have tasted the bread of the truth.
We have drunk the blood of truth:
Here is the cross,
Here is the sacrifice,
Here is the soul.
Now every soul who believes on Him is free.
Say: "Death, where is your victory,
Poverty, misery and hunger—
What can that still do to us?"

Neither angels,
Nor government,
Neither tribulation,
Nor sword,
Nothing, really nothing at all,

Neither depth,
Nor height,
Nor power
Is enough to separate us from the Lord.

Here is the cross,
Here is the sacrifice,
Here is the deed.
This blood has
Freed us from every sin.
Tell me, death, where is your victory?
Here are belief and conviction,
Here is peace.
My God, I have come to You.
Wash my filthy body,
Wash my heart!

And renew my spirit.
My God, I am here.
Here is my body,
Here is my heart,
Here is my soul.

The Move to Malatya

THE PROVINCE capital Malatya is most famous for its apricots. In their dried form these apricots are shipped into all the world. From Kayseri, the ancient Caesarea, one comes on a high road to Malatya, which lies almost 1,000 meters (3,280 feet) above sea level and is surrounded by mountains that are some 2,000 meters (6,560 feet) high. Two of the presidents of the young Turkish Republic, Ismet Inönü and Turgut Özal, came from Malatya, as well as Mehmet Ali Agca, who critically wounded Pope John Paul II in an assassination attempt at St. Peter's Square in Rome in 1981.

When one arrives in Malatya, he has already crossed about two-thirds of Turkey (going west to east) and can easily reach other provinces in the east. With its population of 400,000 the city is not small, and yet, as I noticed once on a bus trip from Izmit to Malatya, lots of people seem to know each other. Those traveling by bus quickly begin talking to one another, as they are among people like themselves. In contrast to the industrial city of Izmit, whose immigrant workers from all corners of Turkey resemble a sort of cultural quilt, the city of Malatya consists of a society that has grown together over a long period of time, has become homogenous, and is therefore rather closed.

In November 2003, Necati and Semse packed their things in their small apartment in Izmir and began the long trip to their new home with their children, who were two and three years old at the time. Semse remembers looking for the prison upon their entrance to Malatya. She expected that Necati's ministry in literature distribution here could also bring him into danger. Both had no doubt, however, that Malatya was the place where God wanted them to be.

Necati and Semse had come to know the Lord in Izmir and had grown in their relationship with Jesus. They went to Malatya conscious that they were sent by the Lord. Here they would also have greater opportunities in ministry and more responsibility. Semse later said that she never looked back to Izmir. That was a supernatural gift of God, but also due to the fact that it gave her satisfaction and joy to work with her husband in directly planting a new church. Necati had more ties to Izmir, his home church, and the fellow believers there. However, he also began the new work zealously.

A few months before Necati and Semse, the South African Christian moved to Malatya with his family, and shortly before the Aydins, Tilmann and Susanne Geske arrived in the apricot city with their children. An English family followed soon afterward. The Christians who had come to Malatya in differing manners decided to have worship services together in their homes, with whoever wanted to join them.

Tilmann and his family had previously lived in Adana for some years. He opened a translation office in Malatya, offering his services to companies and individuals. Necati now worked for Zirve Publishing in the east of Turkey. Normally he would meet with a believer from another city in the east. Together the two would travel to villages and small towns in the company vehicle. They would offer Christian literature to bookstores and magazine stands, small grocery stores, and coffee houses. The latter are the traditional meeting place for Turkish men, who come together to play cards or board games, smoke, watch televised soccer games together, and share personal news, all the while drinking Turkish tea from small glasses.

Necati would meet such people very politely and officially: "Hello, we are from the Zirve Publishing and Dis-

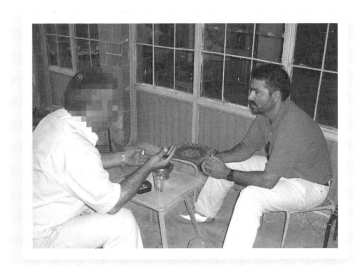

Necati talking about the Christian faith

tribution Company." He and his colleagues knowingly accepted the risk of indignation or rejection. A couple of times they first spoke to the *imam*, the prayer leader at a mosque, so as not to impolitely usurp him.

One day they entered a new village. No one in the coffee house or on the street wanted to accept a New Testament. The fear they had of each other—that is, the peer pressure in the society—seemed to be great. Necati then went to the mosque and the *imam* was open to him. He enthusiastically accepted God's Word saying, "I always wanted to read the *Injil* [New Testament]." This news spread quickly through the village, and suddenly numerous villagers requested Scripture and CDs.

— Necati and his colleagues knowingly accepted the risk of indignation or rejection. —

On his many trips, Necati also visited lonely believers or people who had requested literature from Christian websites. Constant contacts developed and after a time he tried to bring individual believers together into small groups and encourage them in group prayer and Bible study. When he personally visited families, he often asked his wife to travel with him. To visit a family as a family conforms more to Turkish culture.

Again and again the Bible distributors would be picked up by the police or gendarmerie and brought to a police station. Legally, there were no grounds against what the men had done, but that was still not well known in all the provinces. Books, CDs, and audio cassettes were checked; the official permit of the publishing house was examined; and curious questions were asked. Usually, Necati was able to win over the hearts of the police with his polite and respectful demeanor.

One day he had to go to the police station again.

"What is that?" asked the commander harshly while looking at the material being distributed.

Necati used the opportunity to personally relate what was found in the books and why he believed.

The commander politely requested a New Testament, and Necati was more than happy to give him one. This again set a precedent: the other officers were now free to request God's Word, and Necati eagerly supplied the whole police station.

A Divine Chain Reaction

IN MALATYA ITSELF, the newly arrived messengers of Jesus also came into contact with seekers. Meltem, a young woman from Malatya, had visited an aunt in Izmir, who had trusted Jesus there and become a member of a church. After detailed discussions, Meltem asked Jesus to come into her life. When Necati and Semse moved to Malatya, the contact with Meltem was established after a few phone calls. Meltem was not to stay in Malatya very long, but she introduced Semse to her friend Ayse.

A warm friendship developed with this young woman, who lived with her family in a small city outside of Malatya. Ayse was taking a prep course in Malatya for the college entrance exams, which are very important in Turkey. So that she would not have to make the bus trip each day, she liked staying in the city overnight. Soon afterward she would spend two or three nights almost every week at Necati and Semse's. There she was not able to escape detailed explanations of the gospel, which were burning in Semse's passionate evangelistic heart. It took a while for Ayse. She did not take lightly the decision about a life together with Jesus. Semse was discouraged that nothing appeared to take place in her spiritual understanding.

When the Aydins went to western Turkey for a vacation in the summer of 2004, someone called them multiple times on their cell phone. Since the number that appeared in the display was not familiar, Semse simply did not answer. After they returned to Malatya, however, Ayse complained, "Why didn't you answer? I changed my phone number. I wanted to tell you that I have begun to believe on Jesus!"

Ayse became the first link in a divine chain reaction. First of all, she brought her friend Saliha along on her visits to the Aydins. When discussions about spiritual things came about, Saliha mostly just sat there with a very cantankerous look, showing her rejection. However, at some point Semse asked if she could pray for her.

Saliha answered, "I have already begun praying myself!"

Semse encouraged her to surrender her life to Jesus in prayer, and Saliha also entered into a new spiritual world.

In the months that followed, five more young women, mostly students who were preparing for the college entrance exams, came to the Lord and to the newly forming Christian church of Malatya.

Only those who know about how limited young women are in Turkish society—how their families try to shield them from various dangers and how limited their freedom of movement is—can appreciate how great a miracle God performed on these women.

Necati and Semse baptizing new believers in Malatya

Necati and Semse tried to establish contact with the families of these women. Often a deep trust developed when the parents or the big brother saw that a normal and moral Turkish family was before them.

The relationship with these families also demanded sacrifice. A few times Necati and Semse, together with their young children, helped harvest apricots in a village outside of Malatya. In the area surrounding the apricot city of Malatya this was a desperately felt need, an important gesture and an opportunity to talk to each other. Semse very much wanted to tell the mothers of one of the believing women about the gospel of Jesus. For one reason or another it did not work out. Then the women sat together to pit the apricots, and with evangelistic zeal Semse seized the opportunity. "Listen, before we go," she said, "I want to tell you about what we believe."

Even if it was just out of politeness, the mother had to listen.

Suddenly a small mosquito flew into Semse's mouth. *Don't stop talking*, thought Semse, so she swallowed the bug and continued talking.

The woman did not accept the Lord, but Semse heard later how she told others with a certain respect, "That Semse was so zealous to tell me about her faith that she even swallowed a mosquito for it."

Once one of the young women was allowed to travel to a Christian retreat in western Turkey. That may not seem to be anything special from a Western perspective, but in Turkey it indicated how deep the Muslim family's trust in Necati and Semse had become.

Even though the women in Malatya more readily trusted in Jesus, in time interested men gathered around Necati. When the number of believers grew, they started having worship services in two apartments on Sundays. Necati and Tilmann led one of the groups. They really

The Christian fellowship of Malatya at an outdoor meeting

did not think about buying a place for the church gathering. The Bible does not say that a church has to have their own building. For larger evangelistic meetings, such as at Christmas and Easter, they would later rent a meeting room in a hotel. The fellowship with Jesus took place not only on Sundays, but also in everyday life during the week.

For Necati and Semse the young believers were like their own children. Necati again proved to be a gifted organizer and entertainer. He organized bowling or billiard events. Men, women, and children were found on his soccer teams during outings. Weekends they would drive out to the country for a picnic. The young Turks who had up until that time experienced religion as something restrictive and fearful saw in Necati that a life in Jesus is not boring.

Anyone could call at anytime or simply drop by the Aydins. Tea was drunk and games were played, but at the same time the Bible was studied very seriously there. In time Necati and Semse offered marriage courses, and Christians and non-Christians attended. Necati showed them in a practical manner how a Turkish husband would not lose his honor if he sometimes washed the dishes, cooked, or changed diapers. The church in Malatya became very practical.

Sometimes it was hard for Semse to accept that Necati appeared to do more for his spiritual children than for his own. Additionally he was often away on travel for days. However, Semse was also ministering to young Christians full of conviction and was enthused at how God was using her.

The love of God was not only shown to the people of the province of Malatya individually, but on a societal level. With support from Zirve Publishing, Necati determined which projects could be undertaken to contribute to village development in a practical way. In the end he had the idea to renovate village schools. Such a thing is desperately needed in some villages, because the state does not provide the funds for the maintenance of all schools. Necati won over the local official and the school directors for the project. Zirve donated the materials. A group of young people from Western nations used their vacations to do something practical and renovate two schools from the ground up. The young people worked with much enthusiasm and had a lot of fun under Necati's leadership. His hard trials he had experienced as a very young man in construction work were beneficial to him.

Necati and other Christians hoped that they could thus publicly show that, as Christians, they are interested in the good of their state and their city.

A village school that was renovated by Necati's team

Sowing and Reaping of Evil

A S THE FIRST spiritual fruits were being reaped in Malatya, a media campaign against missionaries and all Christians was begun all over Turkey at the end of 2004. An Islamic theology professor was definitely involved. A short time later Rahsan Ecevit, the very politically active wife of the former prime minister Bülent Ecevit, joined the public discussion about missionaries. She openly expressed great concern for her country: Due to the unhindered activities of missionaries, claimed Rahsan Ecevit, many people, especially the young, were being negatively influenced. "*Din elden gidiyor!*—The religion is getting out of hand! I want my country back," she said.

Mrs. Ecevit and her husband were leading the Democratic Leftist Party, whose name expresses their position in the political spectrum. Up until that point Rahsan Ecevit had never appeared as a proponent of Islam. Two years earlier her husband had to leave his position as prime minister after a devastating election loss. His wife probably just wanted to affect the political agenda again with a subject that would interest the general public.

Since the U.S. and its Western allies entered Iraq, the Turkish populace is more quickly inclined to believe evil rumors about the West. The statement of a politician lent the struggle against missionary activities more credibility in the eyes of many Turks and became the impetus for further negative reports on television and in newspapers. Missionary activities and Christianity were spoken about in articles, commentaries, and discussion panels. Sometimes when Christians were interviewed, viewers become interested in Christianity, visited fellowships—and were saved! The main message of the media campaign, however, was: "Be careful! Missionaries are the agents of Western interests and undermine the unity of our country. If the government does not do anything, the people themselves must."

In our small church in Izmit we were on the receiving end of what the press had begun. On the night of December 26, 2004, a rubber and gasoline fire was started in front of our church building. Fortunately, the neighbors put it out in time.

In the weeks following, a local newspaper slandered us with the false report that we would pass out New Testaments on school grounds.

Almost every week people broke the windows and in the end threw a Molotov cocktail toward our meeting room in the upper floor of our building. Fortunately, the device hit the window frame and bounced off.

Because of God's protection, only minor damage was caused by all of these attacks. The incidents were prob-

Headline in a Turkish newspaper: "To do missionary work is a political activity"

ably only meant to be a serious threat. It would be very dangerous to really set the building on fire because the neighborhood was densely populated and linked together by gas lines.

We called the police many times, but it was only after we protested to the assistant governor that the attacks ceased. For some weeks our church building was under 24-hour surveillance.

A few months later someone painted a red swastika on the door of our third-floor apartment (we lived in an eight-story building with about thirty apartments).

When I opened the door the next morning shortly after seven to take my daughter to school, I saw what had been done and on the floor found a handwritten letter threatening us. Somebody had written in a polite and educated manner that we were damaging Turkey and therefore would have to leave the country within a month.

To reinforce this, someone called my cell phone exactly one month later and then two weeks after that and said Mafia-style: "We sent you a letter. The time is up. Please take what we communicated very seriously."

During the second call, Janet, who is Turkish, was sitting next to me. She wanted me to give her the phone, and then she dressed down the caller: "How can you speak to us in this manner? Such a thing is shameful for a Turk."

The man was disgusted that I had let my wife on the phone. Death threats are a man's thing. By the grace of God, and perhaps by the emphatic intervention of my wife, nothing happened to us.

In Malatya Necati and Semse also felt the aggression. Relatively soon after their move, some local newspapers started their negative reporting: "Missionaries are coming to Malatya!"

Some time later the Christians were expecting a large shipment of New Testaments from Istanbul. Somehow news got around that the boxes had arrived at the local package delivery service. Young extreme nationalists then organized a demonstration in front of this office with signs and chants. Bibles were felt to be a threat.

How painful such things must have been for Necati. They were his countrymen, and because he loved them, he wanted to share the most valuable thing he had with them. However, he was being branded an agitator and a destroyer of the country. In February 2005 the local Malatya paper *Bakis* ("View") ran an article about Christians titled "Home Churches in Every Neighborhood." Allegedly they had counted them and came up with forty-eight home churches. That was completely ridiculous, but many believed it. Later, in their statements to the police, Necati's murderers would speak of fifty.

As usual the press soon found a different subject to harp on. However, the seed of rejection and violence that had been sown so abundantly would germinate amply later and lead to even worse acts of violence. The press would soon reap the first fruits of blood.

On February 5, 2006, the Italian Catholic priest Andrea Santoro was shot from behind and killed while praying in his small church in the large city of Trabzon on the Black Sea. Witnesses said that the minor who killed him had called out, "*Allahu Akbar!*" ("Allah is great!") just before shooting.

Not long before he was martyred for Jesus, Necati told his wife that a man had come into his office and made threats as he left. Necati did not appear to take such threats seriously. Or had he rather taken them very seriously and just did not want to cause his wife worry? My brother-in-law did not easily show his thoughts and feelings. In any event he did not let the evident or supposed dangers hold him back from continuing to minister in obedience to God.

Greater Responsibility

IN 2006 NECATI became the pastor in the small but growing Christian church of Malatya. The brothers and sisters who worked together with him recognized that God had gifted him with a "pastor's heart." One of his great strengths was faithfully following up on many different types of church members or Christians who were in areas without fellowship. From time to time I also profited from the encouraging Bible verses that Necati would regularly send to numerous Christian friends as a text message.

The church in Malatya had already decided to begin a partnership with a more established Turkish church. The Kurtulus church fellowship, located in the capital, became the mother church in 2005. ("Kurtulus" means salvation, but is also the name of an area of the city in Ankara.) The pastor of the Kurtulus church, Ihsan Özbek, became a brotherly counselor in questions regarding the Malatya church.

Semse and Necati during their time in Malatya

Necati was not a person to strive for positions of leadership; however, Zirve Publishing also noticed that he had a potential to carry responsibility as a leader. In February 2005 he was made coordinator of the distribution teams of the publishing house. In addition to his own distributions and visitation trips, he now had the job of visiting colleagues in various places in Turkey to plan their work and develop strategies with them.

The young Christian grew more and more into this pastoral responsibility in this area as well. He practiced what his former boss today calls "a great mix of grace and truth." He could identify well with Turkish colleagues and showed them gentle understanding. However, he could also give correction in areas where he thought it was needed. When others were open to his critique, they could feel that he was not "lording it over" them, but rather that Necati was sincere and compassionate.

After Necati's death a former colleague of his made public Necati's last e-mail to his coworkers, in which he spurred them on to devoted love:

Dear brothers,

I wish to embrace all of you with the deep love, the brotherly love, which Christ has recently reminded me of. I kiss you all with a holy kiss. This evening Semse and I have thought about each of you and prayed for all of you. It had given us great joy to think about you and hold you up in our prayers.

Fundamental to the feelings I shared with all of you at least partially in our meeting in Antalya was that I perceive that we need more brotherly love. I have been far away from my physical siblings for years and do not have their love. So I do not also want to lose the love of my spiritual brothers and sisters. I am sure that the love I need and desire is also wanted by you.

I have spoken personally with some brothers. The dissatisfaction and complaints that they expressed were actually the expression of the need for more love. Because they expected the unique love, which we see in Christ, from brothers also, they were not really at fault. However, though we sometimes think and act with the logic that the world encourages us to have, what we really want is "do unto others as you would have them do unto you" —that means to behave with love, with friendship, with sincerity and truth. "Bearing with one another, and forgiving one another, if anyone has a complaint against another; even as Christ forgave you, so you also must do" (Colossians 3:13).

It means a lot that we, who serve the Lord whom we cannot see, forget to show love to our brothers and sisters, those whom we see every day, those whom we have been accustomed to. If we demand our rights from our brother, then we must also give our brother his rights. If we expect respect, we must not forget to show respect, that we not always complain, but rather give thanks. Instead of trying to find fault or a point of vulnerability, we need to all the more consider how we can strengthen. "And above all things have fervent love for one another, for 'love will cover a multitude of sins'" (1 Peter 4:8).

What pleases the Lord the most in our ministry is when we love our brothers and sisters as we love ourselves. When I asked all of you, "Who among you is prepared to give his life for his brothers and sisters?" I did not want to hear an exaggerated epic. I wanted to hear that if it came to this, which would be hard for all of you and me to do, one would say, "I would like to do even this through Him who gives me strength." I do not want to go to war alongside of someone who would abandon me and flee in the time of need. I want to have a brother who would carry me on his shoulders. I want to be armed with love, a love so great that I can carry my brother on my shoulders. My love toward my brother should not wane or be lessened in spite of my brother himself. Rather I pray that I face up to the problem that my brother causes me and that I become perfected in love through it. "But also for this very reason, giving all diligence, add to your faith virtue, to virtue knowledge, to knowledge self-control, to self-control perseverance, to perseverance godliness, to godliness brotherly kindness, and to brotherly kindness love" (2 Peter 1:5–7).

Dear brothers, I know that we, who minister together, sometimes wear each other down and cause each other worry and problems. I have often experienced that it is not easy to act calmly and correctly in such situations. Usually what we do first is to find simple and temporary solutions and maybe put the problem off for a while. However, for a deep-rooted solution what we need to do is to try to solve the problem before the sun sets by coming to each other in a correct and sincere manner in brotherly love, opening our hearts without getting loud. This would certainly be a blessing.

We have been given each other in grace. In the time of a problem this is difficult to understand and accept. However, this is God's plan and the brother is a grace for us. We need to be zealous in this, so that the blessings God wants to give our people and the world through us is not overshadowed by our selfish attitudes. We must use whatever God has given us in the best possible way, so that the opportunities which stem out of our ministries are only blessings. That is then an attitude which is in accordance with our goal: "A new commandment I give to you, that you love one another; as I have loved you, that you also love one another" (John 13:34).

"This is my commandment, that you love one another as I have loved you" (John 15:12).

Dear brothers, I want to encourage all of you and commit all of you to the love of God so that all of you love one another more. I want your love and your joy to be perfected. I want God to fill us with brotherly love; then we will be able to accomplish His will in a worthy manner.

Again I embrace and kiss all of you with love.

Many greetings,

Necati

Since 2006 Ugur Yüksel was also one of Necati's co-workers. He had already become like an older son to Necati and Semse and like an uncle or an older brother for their small children. The Aydins accompanied him through financial difficulties and through the rejection of his family. When he became a worker with Zirve, he moved from Elazig to Malatya and lived with the Aydins for three months until he found his own small apartment.

He had been planning to marry a young woman for a long time, but hindrances always came up: finances, faith, permission of the parents. Necati and Semse sometimes told him jokingly: "You probably will marry in heaven." They did not know how close Ugur was to this unseen reality.

"Do We First Have to Suffer More?"

I N JANUARY 2007 the Armenian journalist Hrant Dink, publisher of the political weekly newspaper *Agos*, was shot to death on the street in Istanbul. The murder was the work of extremist Turkish nationalists. Hrant Dink was no evangelist. For a long time he had lived pretty aloof of the faith of his Christian Armenian people. When he died, it became known that his wife Rachel Dink was a believing Christian and that Hrant Dink had also personally accepted Christ in the last years of his life.

The funeral for Hrant Dink was shown live on many Turkish TV channels, including CNN and NTV. A personal message from the widow Rachel Dink and the sermon of the Armenian-Apostolic Patriarch in Istanbul, Mesrob II Mutafyan, were so permeated with the good news of Jesus Christ that we suddenly noticed that such terrible suffering provided an opportunity for the message of Jesus to be heard. A week later I wrote a letter about this to friends who pray for us:

> It seemed to us that a door was opened for many people, because others spoke credibly in great suffering. Many people here long for words that are authentic and trustworthy. *Do we and the church of Jesus in Turkey first have to suffer more* in order to be more credible witnesses of the mercy of God? How else can people realize that it is not just about an ideological fight over religious ideas but about the message of salvation from eternal death?
>
> Help us by praying for the church in Turkey (including ourselves) to be willing to live sacrificially and even give their lives.

Often I and other Christian coworkers have experienced that the proclamation of the gospel is seen as something political or kind of like a game: "us against them." Some think, *Here come the foreigners who want to push something on us. We must oppose them.*

When a Christian woman, however, spoke of forgiveness and love while standing in front of her husband's casket and proclaimed the message of Jesus, who is also the Savior of Turks, many listeners noticed that the message of hope was also for them.

"Including ourselves" was something I added to the notion of suffering. At the time we had no idea that we would be so directly included only about a month later.

Just a few days before Necati's death I taught at a Bible seminary of Turkish church workers in Ankara. The subject was "The persecution of Christians in the Roman Empire."

God had prepared me even more for the terrible event that would happen on April 18, 2007. Aside from my responsibilities as pastor of the small church in Izmit, I occasionally translated articles or books from English into German. Some months before the murders in Malatya, I began to translate a book by the Canadian Glenn Penner: *In the Shadow of the Cross: A Theology of Persecution.* The author covers the subject of persecution literally from Genesis to Revelation.

I already knew Bible verses about this subject. "Yes, and all who desire to live godly in Christ Jesus will suffer persecution," is how clearly 2 Timothy 3:12 puts it. I can remember that a few decades ago it was fashionable to speak of persecution coming upon us from communism.

As a young theology student I worked in a young adults group of a church. When we covered the subject of persecution, we met in a dark underpass to make it more realistic. However, as a Christian who grew up in Germany I had never really experienced persecution. We tried to illustrate Bible verses that speak of suffering for one's faith in Christ with examples of the small challenges of everyday life or that we might sometimes be laughed at when we give a testimony for Jesus.

When Jesus was preparing His disciples to "bear the cross," He said, "And he who does not take his cross and follow after Me is not worthy of Me. He who finds his life will lose it, and he who loses his life for My sake will find it" (Matthew 10:38,39). Those who heard the words "take his cross" had no doubt seen how those condemned to death were driven to the place of execution. When Jesus said this, He knew that ten of His twelve disciples—all except for Judas Iscariot and John—would literally die as

The author and his brother-in-law

martyrs, that they would be executed because of their faith in Him.

Penner shows profoundly in his book that God did not become the "suffering God" just at the crucifixion of Jesus. In the Old Testament it is revealed to us how God was ready to incur the risk of suffering out of love. He risked and suffered the rejection of His people (Isaiah 65:1,2; Psalm 78:40). He suffered with His people because He showed solidarity with them. God was not unaffected by the slavery that Israel suffered in Egypt (Exodus 2:23,24).

Then God came to this world in Jesus and clearly revealed Himself as a sufferer, and His tasting death was not the first example of His suffering for the salvation of the world. His whole life in our world, which is poisoned by sin and death, was a continual suffering, because He was the Son of God "who knew no sin," who came from the absolute glory of heaven. Then we read that we should be His followers and should live as He did. He included His followers in His life and death (Romans 6:3,4). To be like Jesus in His death is the prerequisite for being like Him in His life (2 Corinthians 4:10). How can we expect to get through this life without having to suffer for Him?

The first human to die on earth was a martyr: Abel died because of his faith. Cain could not stand it that his brother had been accepted by God. The last person who will die before Jesus' return will probably also be a martyr. That is what God's answer given to the martyrs who had already died could mean, after they ask when the just judgment of God will finally come. They are told that "they should rest a little while longer, until both the number of their fellow servants and their brethren, who would be killed as they were, was completed" (Revelation 6:11). When the last martyr dies, Jesus will return.

To be like Jesus in His death is the prerequisite for being like Him in His life.

Inwardly and from His Word God had prepared me for what we would later experience. This does not mean that we lived through all that was to come without any doubt or fear. However, the question "How could God let such things happen?" never entered my mind after Necati's death. Jesus had not left us in the dark about the cost of discipleship.

Faithful Until Death

NECATI AND HIS family visited us in February 2007 while the children had a two-week school vacation. We experienced a lot of beautiful things together. One high point was going sledding on Kartepe, a 1,600-meter- (5,200-foot-) high mountain at the entrance to Izmit. In the evenings we danced in our living room: Necati with his daughter Ester, I with Debora, then Necati with Semse and I with Janet. None of us could dance well, but dancing is an expression of joy in Turkish culture. Ester especially enjoyed being Daddy's "princess." For Elisa, his son, wrestling is a more suitable expression of fatherly affection.

On Sunday Necati preached once again at our small church. After the worship service he had an intensive conversation with Okan, a student who had just started coming to our meetings. Okan later told me that his conversation with Necati had given him important impulses.

A week or two after Necati's sermon, Okan asked me if he could have Necati's phone number. In a chat room of a Christian website, a young man had told Okan that he would like to meet Christians in Malatya. After talking to Necati, I gave Okan only the e-mail address of the fellowship in Malatya. In Turkey I had learned to be careful with personal information. That we had facilitated the contact between Necati and his murderers was something we learned two months later from the police.

Shortly after a brief e-mail correspondence, Necati met personally with the man who said he was interested in Christianity. The name of the young man was Emre Günaydin.

"Semse, I am meeting a young man from the student dorm. He does not seem to be honest. I do not believe that he has a genuine interest in Jesus," Necati once told his wife. Such people often come in contact with Christians.

"At least it is an opportunity for him to hear the saving message of Jesus," Semse told him and encouraged him to use the opportunity. "But be careful not to allow him into the office when you're alone."

Their future murderer spoke with Necati and Ugur a few more times.

On April 8, Easter Sunday, the small church of Malatya held an evangelistic service in a rented room at the Hotel Altin Kayisi, "The Golden Apricot." In Turkey, Christmas and Easter provide Christians excellent opportunities to present information about their faith in a natural way. Visiting Christians on their holiday can be interpreted as a polite gesture, so whoever would visit a church on such an occasion would not be immediately suspected by his friends of being seriously interested in Christianity.

At Easter 2007 numerous Muslim friends accepted the invitation to the service. A short drama explained the resurrection of Jesus. Necati led the program, and a guest speaker from another city gave a short sermon. A few young men, including Emre Günaydin, came to the door, although they were not among those who were invited.

Ugur, who was receiving the guests at the door, was unsure and checked with Necati first. He allowed Emre and his friends to attend the Easter celebration. The young men left the meeting after about half an hour. The church members who met them sensed they were unpleasant and uneasy.

The Easter worship service was a great encouragement for the fifteen to twenty Christians of the Malatya church. Necati and Semse joyfully met with other believers for the evening meal and reflected on the worship service.

Necati speaking in Germany one week before his death

The following day Necati flew to Germany. It was his first time to be invited as a speaker for a Christian conference outside of Turkey. Christians from Germany and other neighboring countries wanted to learn from him how to explain the gospel to people from Turkey. Necati was well prepared for the conference.

Listeners remembered later how sensitive he was in Germany about the necessity of testifying to Turks. As an introduction he presented thoughts which distinguished him and at the same time were his legacy. With respect to 1 Corinthians 9 he said:

> When we serve, we do this for an incorruptible crown. The reward for our service can only be given us by God. When we serve, however, we must do this from the heart, and we must love the people whom we serve. If we want to serve, then we need to stop judging. If we do not judge, then we bless the people.

Necati also told about plans for an evangelistic outreach with young Turkish Christians in the Black Sea region in summer 2007.

Semse, Elisa, and Ester in the meantime were waiting impatiently for their husband and father to return. "When Necati was home, then there was life. When he was away, life seemed to be at a standstill," recollected his wife.

After the conference Necati visited a Turkish-German family close to Frankfurt. He returned home the next Sunday evening, exhausted but happy. He took off work the following Monday and Tuesday. The whole family enjoyed being together. On Tuesday evening Necati played with Elisa and Ester. Wrestling is their favorite activity with their father. Both children were breathing heavily with laughter and joy. Semse also wanted to spend some time with her husband. "I actually had wanted to call him into the living room," she recalled, "but then I had the unexplainable impression not to cut short the children's playing with their father. Later I understood that that was the father's farewell to his children."

Necati as father

While watching TV together later that evening, Necati and Semse happened upon a conservative Islamic channel. A documentary was on which was full of false and aggressive statements about the Christian faith.

Necati turned to Semse: "You know, when I was in the Islamic boarding school, they showed us films like this so that we would be prejudiced against Christianity."

The next morning Semse woke the children alone and brought them to school and kindergarten at about seven. She allowed Necati to sleep in before he returned to his full workload.

When she returned home Necati was half-awake. He hugged Semse and confessed, "I just don't want to get out of bed today." They read the daily Bible verse together from their Scripture devotional. The verse for that day was 1 Samuel 17:45: "Then David said to the Philistine, 'You

come to me with a sword, with a spear, and with a jave-
lin. But I come to you in the name of the LORD of hosts,
the God of the armies of Israel, whom you have defied."
From the New Testament, the verse for the day was 1 John
5:4: "For whatever is born of God overcomes the world.
And this is the victory that has overcome the world—our
faith." Then they read Psalm 86:14,15 together: "O God,
the proud have risen against me, and a mob of violent
men have sought my life, and have not set You before
them. But You, O Lord, are a God full of compassion,
and gracious, longsuffering, and abundant in mercy and
truth." The family devotion time was ended with Necati's
favorite song, "How deep the Father's love for us," and
prayer together.

About 11 o'clock Necati left the apartment. His smile
at the entrance to the elevator on their floor is the last
memory that Semse has of him.

The five young men who planned Necati's murder were
already at the office at about eight o'clock. No one was
there at that hour. They went to the center for Asian
martial arts, which Emre's father ran, and drank coffee.
Before they headed off to the office of Zirve Publishing
to commit murder, each of the young men performed
the Islamic ritual washings and performed a ritual prayer
at an irregular time, which is called a prayer of thanks-
giving.

About 12:30 Semse picked up the children from
school. At about one o'clock she received a call from Ercan
from far-away Izmir: "Somebody has shot at the office!"
Ercan had heard from a believer who had called from
Malatya that something terrible had happened.

"At the moment it was as if someone had poured hot water over my head," Semse recalled.

First she tried to call Necati and then Ugur; there was no answer.

For a few hours she lived in the terrible uncertainty of not knowing what had really happened at the Zirve office. Then she saw on TV how Ugur, still alive but covered with blood, was carried from the office by policemen. She let out a cry of desperation.

Immediately her little daughter Ester came: "Mama, what's wrong? Why did you cry out like that?"

"In order to protect my children, I sealed my heart and threw its key in the ocean," Semse recalled. "But at the same time God laid His hand on my heart and took me away from the incident. It was as if I was observing the events from a higher point of view."

After hours of waiting, she called the police. "Tell me clearly," she pleaded, "whether or not my husband has died!"

"We will let you know as soon as we know something for certain." The police never called.

The certainty that Necati was really dead came from TV news reports. It was confirmed: Necati, Ugur, and Tilmann were brutally murdered.

Not only the police, but also government representatives seemed to avoid Semse. No official came to express his condolences.

The Turkish prime minister expressed his abhorrence for the murders, but Turkish Christians were additionally hurt by one statement he made: "That a German citizen was involved in the incident at the publishing house expands the dimension of the incident, of course." That

Tilmann, Ugur, and Necati

is approximately what Recep Tayyip Erdogan said on TV, and diplomatically, he may have been correct.

However, many Turkish Christians with their background experience thought a different message was being said between the lines: "We have nothing against foreigners who are Christians, and we must protect them, but we respect Christians in our own country less. In that two men turned their backs on Islam and accepted Christianity, we do not want to talk about that."

"I Forgive!"

FOR SEMSE AND her children, a time began that brought them to the absolute limits of their ability to endure. What brought her to her limits was not just the thought that "Necati is no longer here," which like the knives of the murders continually cut into Semse's heart, but that while life goes on, so many decisions had to be made. At the same time, even many Christian friends did not know what to do or say in such a situation and sometimes hurt Semse.

Not only did many believers start coming to Malatya to help and to console right after the news of the murders, but an army of reporters soon arrived too.

Semse and Susanne, the wife of Tilmann Geske, very soon announced publicly, "We forgive the murderers!" Naturally they both could only say this in faith without regard for their own feelings; but they were credible. This found an enormous resonance in newspapers and TV and in web pages.

"I Forgive!"

The editorial writer of a large Turkish newspaper said in effect a couple of days later, "The murderers wanted to hinder the activities of the missionaries. But what these women have facilitated in a few days by their statements is something that a thousand missionaries could not have done in a thousand years."

To express forgiveness in such a situation runs contrary to many Turks' sense of justice. Some people showed their displeasure that anyone could forgive such brutal murderers. Does that mean that these ladies did not really love their own husbands?

"It was not easy for me to say that I forgive the killers," Semse said later at the memorial service. "To be honest, my heart is broken and my life feels shattered. I really loved Necati. He was the love of my life, my closest friend. But there is no one I love more than Jesus. Only because of this, I can bear it."

Tilmann's widow Susanne Geske and Semse

People who do not believe on Jesus cannot understand that this sort of forgiveness is a supernatural gift of God. Forgiveness does not include the wish that these murderers should be spared earthly punishment. Forgiveness means to forgo one's own feelings of vengeance and to bless the murderers in the name of Jesus.

"My greatest wish," Semse said, "is that the murderers repent from their hearts, as the apostle Paul was broken before Jesus, and then as Necati was, that they become witnesses to the forgiveness of God. Then Necati's death will not have been in vain."

Semse felt that she could not remain in Malatya at that time. Immediately after Necati's burial, which took place in Izmir, the city of their love, she and her children moved to Izmit to live with us.

Malatya remained in their hearts, however. Semse kept in active contact with the Christians in Malatya and tried, in spite of her own pain, to encourage her "spiritual children" to stay with Jesus. She used the opportunity of the opening trial of the murderers in November 2007 to visit Christians in Malatya.

Semse did not remain in her own self-pity, but rather became involved in our small church in Izmit with all her strength.

To become still inwardly was hard for her in Izmit, too. The murderers of Necati, Ugur, and Tilmann had said that they had also wanted to kill me, the brother-in-law of Necati. They had planned to come to Izmit after the murders in Malatya. Because of this I was given a personal bodyguard by the Turkish police. So it became

Semse at Necati's grave

obvious to Semse that Izmit is also a dangerous place for Christians.

Naturally Semse and her children went through various emotionally difficult times in dealing with their trauma. Later they were able to have intensive Christian therapy.

Through it all, it remained clear to Semse that she could not imagine anything else except to continue following Jesus Christ. Despite all the pain, she feels that her beloved husband was honored by Jesus in his special death as a martyr. "Now, God has taken him back," Semse said. "He is the one who gives and takes away. So how can I be angry with the God who is over everything?"

Does Persecution Bring About Revival?

JESUS SAID, "Truly, truly, I say to you, unless a grain of wheat falls into the earth and dies, it remains alone; but if it dies, it bears much fruit" (John 12:24, NASB). He was not just speaking of His own death here, but also of the martyrdoms of many of His followers.

After the deaths of the three believers in Malatya, has there been any spiritual fruit? Every now and then we have either experienced or heard of concrete fulfillments of this promise of Jesus.

Shortly after the murders some Turks who were impressed about what had happened said "yes" to a life with Jesus at a worship service in another large Turkish city.

A young man in Malatya, whom we later met personally, had already heard about Jesus from Christians from Malatya. When Necati died, he suddenly realized how serious and credible this message is. He turned to Christ in a radical way.

Inscription on the grave: (front) The first Christian Turkish Martyr, Massacre of Malatya, 18.4.2007. (side) Jesus said: "Whoever believes in Me will live, even though he dies."

A Turkish pastor in southern Turkey began to be terribly ashamed after the death of his brothers in the faith. As a government employee he had hesitated to officially change his religious affiliation on his identity card (to Christian instead of Muslim), although it was possible. He thought, *That could be disadvantageous.* Now he was pricked to the heart: "These brothers were prepared to die for their faith, and I am not ready to be officially identified with Jesus." After "Christian" was finally printed on his identity card, he told his church and was surprised to hear that some other members had done the same thing without having spoken about it.

We have heard about spiritual repercussions in other countries following the martyrdom of the three believers. A lady from Germany wrote to tell us that she had decided to commit herself totally to Jesus after hearing the reports of Malatya.

The worldwide solidarity of the Church of Jesus is a great encouragement in this situation. E-mails, letters, donations, and visits show that in many countries Christians have begun to pray more intensely for Turkey and especially for the families of the martyred men.

We have heard from Afghanistan, India, Israel, and many other countries how the incident in Malatya had a great resonance.

Persecution does not automatically bring revival. Rather, persecution is a crisis that demands our answer.

Revival? We have not seen much of that in Turkey. Our church in Izmit got smaller. Christians or those who were about to make a decision stayed away, because the price for following Jesus appeared too high. We have heard similar things about other areas in Turkey. Persecution does not automatically bring revival. Rather, persecution is a crisis that demands our answer. Perhaps God is using the murders for purification: Some Christians decided to trust Christ completely. Those who had previously come just because it was different, or because they could profit through contact with foreign Christians, now knew that suffering for the sake of Christ was a realistic possibility. But this purification of the fellowships in Turkey is hardly measurable even now.

We have the promise of Jesus, and because of this the great assurance that the martyrdoms of Necati, Ugur, and Tilmann will produce spiritual fruit. The grains of wheat that have died will not remain alone. We believe that in April 2007 we were very near to the reality of the Kingdom of God, where the directives of Jesus which always included suffering occurred; where there were martyrs who really bore the cross; where three men as followers of Jesus literally were as lambs going to slaughter and remained faithful to Him until death.

Somewhere in Turkey two little Necatis are growing up. Their parents were Muslims like Necati and found Christ like he did. They gave this name to their newborn babies to remember my brother-in-law. One of the fathers told me, "I want my son to bring the gospel to many people in Turkey, like the murdered brothers did." Apart from the "biological Necatis," we think of the "spiritual Necati"—the young man mentioned at the beginning of this chapter who is so excited to tell other students about Jesus. God alone knows how many other "Necatis" are growing up just now in this great country hidden from our eyes.

The Responsibility of Christians in Germany and Beyond

TURKS HAVE A good feel for symbolic gestures, and I think that God also uses symbolic messages.

In Malatya two Turkish Christians died—one of whom (Necati) was from a Sunni family, which is the main Islamic group; the other (Ugur) from the special Islamic group of the Alevis—and a German messenger of Jesus (Tilmann) died with them in Turkey.

Shortly after the murders my prayer was that we rightly understand God's symbolism in this, that we as foreigners who want to serve in Turkey understand that love and devotion are required—if necessary, to the point of death. And that Turkish Christians and others in Turkey understand that among the foreigners are those who did not come to Turkey as delegates of their nations or representatives of Western civilization, or because they can live more comfortably here, but they serve in Turkey simply because they want to obey the command of Jesus. At least one of the foreign Christians went this way to the end.

That God permitted two Turks and a German to be martyrs for Jesus is also a message for Christians in Germany.

Germans and Turks have special historical ties. Whether or not it pleases us, Turkish friends have told me again and again that we were allies with each other in the First World War, and they derived a certain nearness and trust from this. Since the 1960s more and more people came to Germany as guest workers from Turkey. Today there are thought to be almost 3 million people from Turkey in Germany. Our sovereign God has thus placed a special opportunity directly at the feet of His Church in Germany, to bring this great people nearer His love through Jesus in word and in deed.

Despite these historical ties between Germans and Turks, there are fewer Germans who want to serve Jesus in Turkey than there are Americans or Koreans. I know that dramatic gestures are foreign to Germans, yet in Malatya we have a "blood brotherhood" in its purest and most hallowed form. Not in order to wage war together again, but rather that the German and Turkish church of Jesus, as equals, bring the gospel to this important country.

It is no longer the case only that German Christians go to Turkey, but also that a few Turkish Christians come to Germany to witness. Days before his death, Necati himself called on Christians in Germany to proclaim the gospel to Turks in love.

All of this will not be easy. We are so different. Misunderstandings occur so easily, even among people who are dedicated to Jesus. However, we cannot return to the time before April 18, 2007—neither in Turkey nor in Germany.

I pray that the bold witness of Necati, Ugur, and Tilmann will challenge the body of Christ worldwide. We are called not only to pray for Christians who are suffering, but to remember those who are mistreated as if we ourselves were suffering (see Hebrews 13:3). More than this we are challenged to commit our own lives to Jesus Christ as a "living sacrifice." In our Western societies protecting our own lives often seems to be the highest value. But for disciples of Jesus, the word of our Master is of even higher value. He wants us to be *faithful until death*.

Conclusion

HAVE I DEPICTED Necati too positively? Surely my brother-in-law would have wanted me to tell more about his weaknesses.

We also witnessed arguments between Necati and Semse. I could have tried to highlight the limits of his personality. Necati, for example, found it difficult to reveal his own hardships to other brothers in the faith. Certainly, I could find areas in his life where we could have said he still needed healing.

Although I knew Necati better, I can say this is true of Tilmann and Ugur also: their lives reflected a whole-hearted commitment to God. Necati was a man whose heart was with Jesus. This is something that cannot be related in an exhaustive description of his character, but is a cumulative impression. Though he was not a super-hero, I am convinced that I was close to a "man after God's own heart."

Possible character weaknesses are not important now anyway. Today he stands before God's throne and is among "the souls of those who had been slain for the word of God and for the testimony which they held" (Revelation 6:9)—and is perfected forever.

I would be happy to learn about your impressions and thoughts while reading this book. You may communicate with me by e-mail at: meinschwager@gmail.com.

Conclusion

To Necati, my brother-in-law, my brother,

As I write tears come to my eyes. I miss you. You are missed by your family, and you are missed by me and by many Christians in Turkey whose lives you have touched. However, I am proud of you and of Jesus, who took hold of and has perfected your life. I will be proud if Jesus grants me the honor of gathering part of the fruit of your death in Turkey.

One day when we will all be together worshiping before God and His sacrificial Lamb Jesus, then you will be among the people whom I would like to stand near in the great choir of the redeemed. Not only because of your strong and beautiful voice, but because of the genuineness of your life, which has made it easier for me to believe on Jesus and to arrive at that great final concert.

Thank you, Necati!

May Death Be Near Us

I say: May death be near us!
Isn't it always near anyway?
I go, without a farewell,
Without being able to tell the one, who I love,
Without having become full
Of love, truth, beauty, and what is good,
I run in every moment of my life,
To arrive at any moment at the goal, in eternity.

May death be near us!

I go to the end of the road,
In silence, while I speak,
At the point, where I burn.
In the end all of my calculations
Are under my eyelids.
With the pulse of the heart, which lets live,
With breathing every day,
With each sunset,
When winds fall silent,
When the roses wither,
At birth, to live,
Life is always headed toward death.
If we live to die,
If death is a part of us,
Then do not be afraid of death.
Embrace it, surround it,
Hold it by the hand, never to let it go.

May death be near us!

Conclusion

Be the last word on my lips.
Do not let yourself hear, do not speak, do not go away.
In the end, death, take me into your arms,
To come together without separating us.
Embrace me.
I come and sob: Hallelujah!

Translated from the volume of Necati's poems, *Necati Aydin: Benim Adim Göklerde Yazili! ("My Name Is Written in the Heavens!")* (Istanbul: Gercege Dogru Kitaplari, 2008), pp. 46–47, "Ölüm bize yakin olsun."

The Persecuted Church

THE VOICE OF THE MARTYRS has many other books, videos, brochures, and other products to help you learn more about the persecuted church. In the U.S., to order materials or to receive our free monthly newsletter, call (800) 747-0085 or write to:

The Voice of the Martyrs
P. O. Box 443
Bartlesville, OK 74005-0443
www.persecution.com
thevoice@persecution.com

If you are in Canada, England, Australia, New Zealand, or South Africa, contact:

Australia:
The Voice of the Martyrs
P.O. Box 250
Lawson NSW 2783
Australia

Website: www.persecution.com.au
Email: thevoice@persecution.com.au

Canada:
The Voice of the Martyrs
P.O. Box 608
Streetsville, Ontario L5M 2C1
Canada

Website: www.persecution.net
Email: thevoice@persecution.net

New Zealand:

The Voice of the Martyrs
P.O. Box 5482
Papanui, Christchurch 8542
New Zealand

Website: www.persecution.co.nz
Email: thevoice@persecution.co.nz

South Africa:

Christian Mission International
P.O. Box 7157
1417 Primrose Hill
South Africa

Email: cmi@icon.co.za

United Kingdom:

Release International
P.O. Box 54
Orpington BR5 9RT
United Kingdom

Website: www.releaseinternational.org
Email: info@releaseinternational.org

Wolfgang Haede

Born in Germany, Wolfgang Haede and his Turkish wife, Janet, have one daughter, Debora. After graduating from a theological seminary, Wolfgang worked in a Christian rehabilitation center for people with drug problems. Feeling called to reach people from Turkey with the good news about Jesus, he started ministering to Turks in Germany together with his wife. Since 2001 the Haede family has been living and serving in western Turkey. For a couple of years they pastored a small evangelical Turkish church in Izmit, near Istanbul. A special focus of Wolfgang's ministry is to help provide good theological training for Turkish Christians.